your GIRL

A Bible Study for Mothers of Teens

{ VICKI COURTNEY }

LifeWay Press®

ISBN: 1-4158-3098-3

Dewey Decimal Classification Number: 306.874
Subject Heading: MOTHERS AND DAUGHTERS \ CHRISTIAN LIFE \ GIRLS

Printed in the United States of America

Student Ministry Publishing
LifeWay Church Resources
One LifeWay Plaza
Nashville, Tennessee 37234-0174

We believe the Bible has God for its author; salvation for its end; and truth, without any mixture
of error, for its matter and that all Scripture is totally true and trustworthy.
The 2000 statement of *The Baptist Faith and Message* is our doctrinal guideline.

Contents

TEACHING PLANS

⟲ ⟲ *About Vicki Courtney* ⟲ ⟲

VICKI COURTNEY is the founder of Virtuous Reality Ministries® which reaches over 150,000 girls and mothers each year. A mother of three teens, she seeks to provide teens and their parents with the tools necessary to navigate today's culture. Her online magazine for teen girls, *virtuousreality.com*, has attracted visitors from all 50 states and 30+ countries. She has also developed *virtuealert.com* as a parent's resource tool to understanding today's rapidly changing teen culture. She is a national speaker and the best-selling author of several books including, *Your Girl: Raising a Godly Daughter in an Ungodly World* and its counterpart, *Your Boy: Raising a Godly Son in an Ungodly World*, as well as magabooks for teen girls, *TeenVirtue: Real Issues, Real Life...A Teen Girl's Survival Guide* and *TeenVirtue 2: A Teen Girl's Guide to Relationships*. Vicki is also the author of several popular Bible studies including, *The Virtuous Woman*, and *Get A Life*. More information about Vicki can be found at *www.VickiCourtney.com*.

⟲ ⟲ *How to Use This Resource* ⟲ ⟲

Bible Study

Each chapter contains a Bible study. This study is not intended as five days of homework or study each week. You probably can complete the work in one 30- to 45-minute time frame. You can do the Bible study all in one sitting, or you can choose to complete a section at a time. However, if you choose this route, you may need to do some rereading each day so you know where you were when you left off. Like a good book, you don't want to lose the plot when you put it down for a while.

Talking Points

Throughout this Bible study, we've provided "talking points" for you and your daughter. These are intended to help engage your daughter in conversation about the topics. You may want to sit down with your daughter at a specific time to talk with her about these battles she's facing. However, you might find it more productive to "slip in" these discussions within everyday conversation, such as a trip in the car to soccer practice or while setting the table. Sometimes talking with your daughter about these issues will be easy; other times, it will be difficult. The nature of the topic may dictate how you approach the subject. Whenever you choose to initiate a dialogue, strive for honesty and vulnerability. It's OK to share times you've made mistakes. It's also OK to say, "I don't know" when your daughter asks a question you can't answer. You're not perfect, and your daughter knows that. Just be real. If you've never really engaged your daughter in conversations like these, that's OK. This is a good starting point. Don't feel like you are supposed to be perfect. You're building a relationship with your daughter, and that takes time.

Small-Group Study Plans

In the back of this book are suggestions for leading a small group of mothers through this study. You may learn a great deal from reading this book, doing the Bible study for each week, and listening to the material on the audio CD. However, meeting weekly with other women can be a source of great encouragement, support, and accountability that would be lacking in doing this Bible study solo. You probably know other women who would benefit from this study—women in your Sunday School class, mothers of your teen's friends, coworkers, women in your carpool, and others.

Each week's small-group study plan contains several elements including a Bible study, reflection on the material in this member book, and discussion based on the DVD. Your group may find that an hour is not enough time to cover all the material. If you need to spend two weeks on one topic, that is OK. The goal is not finishing the study within the eight weeks. The goal is to help prepare, challenge, and encourage moms as they strive to grow a godly daughter in an amoral culture.

Audio CD

Inserted in the back of this book is an audio CD. On it you will hear segments of the trade book *Your Girl: Raising a Godly Daughter in an Ungodly World,* read by the author Vicki Courtney. This CD does not contain the book in its entirety. Rather, it features parts from the book that are not contained in either this Bible study or the DVD segments.

↶◎ *Introduction* ◎↷

The drama surrounding the birth of my second child should have been my clue that life would never be the same. On a Saturday afternoon, several days before my due date, I mentioned to my husband, Keith, that I was experiencing scattered contractions. He dismissed it as false labor and discouraged me from calling my doctor. We had made several unnecessary trips to the hospital before. Keith, no doubt, was having flashbacks of our last hospital visit where he got to sleep upright in a metal chair while they monitored my false contractions throughout the night.

By Saturday evening my contractions were coming more regularly, at a safe six minutes apart. Once again Keith discouraged me from calling my doctor. As the contractions continued to close in, I trusted my instincts and called my doctor. Keith, still doubting, begrudgingly got into the car. After dropping off our two-year-old son at a friend's house, we began the 30-minute drive to the hospital. The contractions were coming at a regular three minutes apart and had taken on a level of pain that was somewhat reminiscent of the final stages of labor with my first child. I made a note to self: banish husband to couch for remainder of marriage. By the time we neared the hospital, Keith had turned on the hazard lights and was running every red light. I'm not sure if the petrified look on his face was due to fear of my coming wrath or fear of delivering our second child on the highway.

Finally, my husband squealed into the emergency entrance of the hospital, and I was immediately whisked away in a wheelchair. Keith raced to park the car. I knew it was serious when the nurse bypassed the station where I was to fill out the obligatory mounds of paperwork and screamed, "I need to get her into a room!" No sooner had the nurse put me in a bed, my water broke; and my contractions were coming one on top of another. At that point I was consumed with only one thought. I wish I could say it was a thought concerning the fact that my husband might miss the birth of our second child while parking the car, but instead it boiled down to this: epidural! I want my epidural!

Normally I am one tough woman, but when it comes to natural childbirth and being an "earth woman," forget it. The epidural I had received prior to the birth of my first child had left me extolling the virtues of modern medicine. Now, during my second delivery, Keith finally made it into the room as the nurse was calmly reassuring me that both my doctor and the anesthesiologist were just down the hall with another patient. "You are next on their list. Don't worry, there is plenty of time for an epidural." Just as she finished her last sentence, she glanced over to check my progress and screamed, "Oh no! The baby is crowning!" With that, she looked at my husband (who was wiping his brow, still shaken from the car ride) and screamed, "Quick! Go find me a doctor!" Now I don't know about you, but a panicked nurse who is relying on a panicked father to find a doctor is not reassuring.

I could hear my husband in the hallway stammering, "Uh, we need a doctor. My wife . . ." Before he could finish his sentence, in rushed a man wearing blue jeans and a button-down-collar shirt. Great, I thought. He's recruited a father out of the waiting room to deliver our child. I sure hope he's seen enough episodes of ER to pull this off. The stranger barely had time to put on the sterile gloves before I made the final push. With that, he held my baby up, and I heard my husband say, "It's a girl! We have a daughter!" I could hardly contain my joy as a smile covered my face.

The stranger in street clothes asked Keith to cut the cord, and I vaguely remember thinking, *If these two amateurs leave my beautiful princess with a three-inch outie, I'll never forgive them.* Sensing my panic, the stranger informed me that he was an obstetrician and had stopped by the hospital to check on patients before going out to dinner. After cutting the cord (leaving a beautiful innie, by the way), he handed my daughter over to the nurse, who wrapped her tightly in a blanket and laid her on my chest. Of course, my first thought was that she was the most beautiful thing I had ever seen. In truth, she looked more like a little blue Smurf, due to her fast trip through the birth canal. All the same I counted 10 fingers and 10 toes and winced at the piercing set of lungs that left no doubt as to who was in charge. After inspecting my princess, I looked up at Keith and said, "We have a daughter. I got my girl." Drama over, right? Wrong. It was only just beginning.

In that first year I would often stand over her crib and watch her while she slept. I would talk to God and plead with Him to spare her from some of the painful mistakes I had made during my growing up years. Would she love me? Would she even like me? Would we become lifelong friends? Would she come to love the God I serve? Sure, I had many of the same questions with the birth of my son, Ryan; but somehow, this was different. It would be Keith's responsibility to model to Ryan, as well as to our third child, Hayden, what it means to be a godly man. It would be my responsibility to model to Paige what it means to be a godly woman. Could I do it? Was I up for the task?

I Am Mother, Hear Me Roar!

Today's culture makes it difficult to raise a godly daughter. In fact, today's culture leaves me furious. I can't take it any longer. If I continue to be subjected to the lewd subtitles on the covers of women's fashion magazines every time I stand in the grocery store checkout line, I just may give up eating. "Whispers, Oohs or Yahoos—Wouldn't You Like to Know What He Thinks about Your Lovemaking Noise Level?" How about, "Make Him Lust for You—the Most Erotic Way to Unhook Your Bra and More Tantalize-Him Tricks" or "Sex on the Brain—What the Guys in Your Office Are Really Thinking," "His 126 Secret Sex Thoughts—the Dastardly Details Racing through His Mind Right Now!" and "G-Spots, C-Spots, and Now, V-Spots." What's left? Have we made it through the alphabet yet? Have women become nothing more than sex-starved junkies looking for a fix? The focus of these articles is always the same: use your "lust-abilities" to get your man. Don't expect him to look your way unless you can belly dance in the bedroom or tantalize him with the latest snag-a-man technique.

Teen fashion magazines, which are targeted to young impressionable 13- to 17-year-old girls, are not much better. Examples of subtitles are: "Be a Guy Magnet," "Make the First Move . . . P.S. He's Waiting," "Get That Guy! How to Give the 'Look of Love' Plus Three Other Tricks That'll Have Him Dying to Get Close to You," "Twenty-two Jeans That Scream 'Nice Butt!'" Or how about these: "Swimsuits That'll Make Him Say, 'Hello!'" or "Kiss Him! How to Make the First Move." Another one is, "Best Bottoms for Your Butt: Tops That Tease and Please." No doubt the magazines are a dream come true for every teenage boy in America with raging hormones. Suffice it to say, I'm fed up with the negative influences of our culture on women. The magazines, however, are only part of the problem. Add television, movies, and music; and our daughters are bombarded with smut from the moment they wake up to the moment they go to bed. As someone who is in the trenches of ministry to preteen and teen girls, not to mention their mothers, I am witnessing firsthand the devastating consequences our provocative culture is having on women both young and old.

I recall one devastated mother at a conference at which I spoke. She sobbed on my shoulder as she shared about a sleepover her middle-school daughter had attended. The popular group of boys had called the girls in the middle of the night. Nothing different from the middle-school sleepovers of my day, I initially thought. Unfortunately, these boys had been surfing porn sites prior to calling the girls, and they wanted to try out their new knowledge of "phone sex." Not your average sleepover from my day. One at a time the boys described in graphic detail what they would do to each girl, if ever given the opportunity. Don't think something like this cannot happen to your daughter. These were "church kids."

For those of us who are committed to raising our daughters to be godly young women, we have a daunting task before us. My generation was subjected to its share of negative messages but nothing that compares to the constant barrage of negative messages our daughters endure today at the hands of television, movies, music, magazines, and the Internet. The negative messages in my day tended to come at the hands of a few groups that constituted the minority voice. Unfortunately, many of the groups that once had a minority voice have now become the popular voice of the day.

The good news is that Christians are the majority in this country. The bad news is that we have apparently lost our voice because we have become the silent majority. If something is not done to counteract the negative influences in our culture, I fear we could lose an entire generation of young women to the ways of the world. Let's not fool ourselves into thinking the damage will only be short-term. If we don't find our voice and use it to speak out against the negative influences of our culture, our daughters will be molded by the voice of the day. The resulting damage will produce fallout that will carry over into our daughters' marriages and into their motherhood, thus impacting generations to come.

What Are "the Times"?

Why is it important for us to take an active role in raising our daughters to be godly women? That a quick glance at our world today. Once you've read the following, that question will have been answered.

ISSUES FACING TODAY'S FAMILIES

- Born-again Christians are just as likely to have been divorced as are non-born-again adults. More than 90 percent of such born-again Christians experienced their divorce after becoming born-again.[1]
- In 2000, 33 percent of all babies were born to unmarried women, compared to 3.8 percent in 1940.[2]
- Sex is the number one searched for term on the Internet today.[3]
- Adult bookstores now outnumber McDonald's restaurants in the U.S. by a ratio of 3:1.[4]
- Two out of every three shows on TV contain sexual content.[5]

ISSUES DIRECTLY FACING OUR DAUGHTERS

- The number one wish for girls ages 11 to 17 is to be thinner.[6]
- One study of Saturday morning toy commercials found that 50 percent of commercials aimed at girls spoke about physical attractiveness while none of the commercials aimed at boys referred to appearance.[7]
- Thirty percent of high school seniors reported having at least five drinks in a row in the previous two weeks.[8]
- Nationwide, 46 percent of students in grades 9 through 12 have had sex.[9]
- Nearly 35 percent of all young women in the U.S. become pregnant at least once before reaching the age of 20—almost 850,000 each year.[10]
- Eighty-three percent of teens say that moral truth depends on the situation.[11]
- Dating on college campuses is all but obsolete, having been replaced by a hookup culture, where a guy and a girl get together for some form of physical encounter (ranging from kissing to having sex) with no expectation of anything further.[12]

Do these statistics frighten you? Or has the world we live in numbed you to the reality of the dark world through which our daughters must navigate? Unfortunately, most of us have been lulled to sleep gradually to the point that the previous statistics don't shock, scare, or worry us. Over time the world's influence has slowly seeped into our thinking, shifting our mind-sets and weakening our resolve. However, as Christian mothers, we {11} must awaken from our slumber, equip ourselves for battle, and refuse to allow the world to take our girls by the hand and lead them through life. If we don't take action, be assured, our daughters will be indoctrinated into the popular thinking of the day.

As I see the landscape before me, I am convinced of my role to counter the culture's influence and take a stand for my daughter's sake. While our culture teaches that a person's soul can be full and whole by indulging in everything from carnal pleasures to intellectual prowess, I will teach my daughter that all people have a huge, gaping hole within their heart that can only be satisfied by the perfect love of Jesus Christ. While culture teaches girls to take charge of their lives, their bodies, and their futures, she will be reminded that Jesus liberated all women more than two thousand years ago when He died on the cross for our sins. His movement never has been and never will be quenched as it continues to spread to every corner of the world. As a leader, Jesus is credible, is reliable, and has a glowing list of references that attest to His life-changing power. He doesn't change the rules to match the times. He is the same yesterday, today, and forever. My daughter will be encouraged to keep these truths in mind as she encounters other young ladies who have fallen prey to the negative influences of the culture and have attempted to fill the huge holes in their hearts with everything but the unfailing love of God.

Our girls are in desperate need of new direction. Our culture has failed them. They long for rest in their souls. We have the answer. It's time for you and me to stop relegating the spiritual and moral development of our daughters to a culture that is neither godly nor moral. For the sake of our daughters, let's not rest until we see it happen.

Take the Challenge

Over the next eight weeks, you will be confronted with six major issues teen girls face: conformity, self-esteem, modesty, purity, boys, and girl politics. As you learn about how these issues impact your daughter, you will be challenged to evaluate how these issues impact your own life. While these issues will manifest themselves differently in the various arenas in your life (your daughter is tempted to go with the crowd at a party; you're tempted to follow the crowd at the office, for example), the root issues will be remarkably applicable for you even as an adult.

You need to be honest with yourself and with God as you read, journal, pray, and talk to other women. If you are to take seriously your role as a spiritual leader for your daughter, you must make sure you are providing a Christlike model for her to follow. I'm not asking you to be perfect; I'm asking you to evaluate your life honestly to see how you might need to grow in each of these areas yourself. As God works in and through your life to better reflect His character and design for your life, you'll be better equipped to help your own daughter.

A Mother's Prayer

On a recent evening I stood again over her bed and watched my now 15-year-old princess sleep. Her crib has long since been replaced with a contemporary cast-iron daybed. Gone was the little girl with the soft curls. Lying before me that evening was a teenager with a wispy blonde ponytail, notes from her friends pasted on the wall above her headboard, and her cell phone, iPod®, and driver's permit resting on the nightstand. Many of the questions I had petitioned to God while standing over her crib in earlier years had been answered. Yes, she loves me. She even likes me and will, on occasion, even hug me and tell me so. Yes, she loves Jesus ... for now. But what about tomorrow? And the next day? And the days to come? Could she continue to stand firm in a culture absent of virtue? In the end, would I succeed in my call to raise my daughter to be a godly woman?

As I glanced around her room, most everything was different, yet a few things remained the same. Lying near my 10th-grade princess was "Nanny Beth," her stuffed bear from infancy, and her mother still prayed. That evening my prayers took on a more urgent tone as I realized that the time remaining in the nest would soon expire. She was slowly getting her wings, and she would soon take flight. Once again I was overwhelmed with the magnitude of the responsibility I had been given. With that thought, I knelt beside her bed and prayed over my daughter "Thank you, Lord, for trusting me with this priceless treasure. May I be a model of strength and godliness to her as she grows more and more in Your likeness. May she come to love You more than life itself." Quietly, I got up and kissed her softly on the cheek and whispered one final plea: "Father, help me raise my daughter to be Your girl." May that be your prayer as well.

{ 13 }

1. "Born Again Adults Less Likely to Co-Habit, Just as Likely to Divorce." Barna Research Group, press release, 6 August 2001.
2. Barbara Kantrowitz and Pat Klingert, "Unmarried, with Children," Newsweek, 28 May 2001, 46.
3. "Alexa Research Finds 'Sex' Popular on the Web" Business Wire, 14 February 2001.
4. Kerby Anderson and Perry Brown, "The Peril of Pornography," American Tract Society.
5. "Sex on TV: Content and Context," Kaiser Family Foundation, 1999.
6. Jean Holzgang, "Facts on Body and Image," 14 April 2000, Just Think Foundation, http://www.justthink.org/bipfact.html.
7. "Media's Effect on Girls: Body Image and Gender Identity," National Institute on Media and the Family, 2002, http://www.mediafamily.org/facts/facts_mediaeffect.shtml.
8. "America's Children: Key National Indicators of Well-Being, 2001." Forum on Child and Family Statistics, 40, http://www.childstats.gov/ac2001/ac01.asp.
9. Youth Risk Behavior Surveillance System, Centers for Disease Control and Prevention, 2002.
10. S. K. Henshaw, "U.S. Teenage Pregnancy Statistics with Comparative Statistics for Women Aged 20-24." The Alan Guttmacher Institute, 2003.
11. "Americans Are Most Likely to Base Truth on Feelings," Barna Research Group, press release, 12 February 2002.
12. Independent Women's Forum Study, "Hooking Up, Hanging Out, and Hoping for Mr. Right."

The Choice Before You

"**I**T IS MY CONVICTION that many mothers will occupy a higher position in God's kingdom than many prominent Christian leaders whom we might expect to find in places of greater honor. Think of some of the great men of the Bible like Moses, Samuel, and Timothy. Where would they have been had it not been for their praying, Spirit-led mothers? Think of Augustine, John Newton, and the zealous Wesleys; their names may never have lighted the pages of history had it not been for the blessed influence of godly mothers!

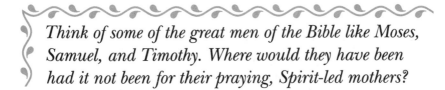

> *Think of some of the great men of the Bible like Moses, Samuel, and Timothy. Where would they have been had it not been for their praying, Spirit-led mothers?*

The simple prayers from our infant lips were but echoes from our mother's heart. Can we ever forget the soft caresses of those hands of blessing on our heads as we knelt by our beds? Can we fail to remember her night vigils, her seasons of intercession, her well-marked Bible, and her words of admonition? Her actions spoke eloquently of Him who taught us of the greater love of God.

What a tragedy to neglect the counsel of a godly mother! What eternal consequences to reject her God. . . . 'Do not forsake the law of your mother' (Prov. 1:8)". —Henry G. Bosch[1]

President John Quincy Adams once said, "From all that I had read of history and government of human life and manners, I had drawn this conclusion, that the manners of women were the most infallible barometer to ascertain the degree of morality and virtue of a nation."

This is certainly a humbling thought, given the current absence of virtue in our culture. Yet, rather than resolve ourselves to the times with an attitude that says, "It's too little too late," I suggest we rise up to the challenge and give it everything we've got. If President Adams was right and the manners of women have a direct impact on the morality and virtue of a nation, then as mothers of daughters, we have received a high calling.

God has placed a task before us as mothers to impact the next generation of women, starting with our daughters. In a culture that esteems success, wealth, knowledge, and power for women, motherhood fails even to make the ballot when it comes to noteworthy aspirations. This is in spite of the fact that no greater influence exists than that of a mother to her child. If we are to raise godly seed for the next generation, we must devote ourselves to this high calling with purpose and determination. We cannot abdicate the spiritual training of our children to the church, a private Christian school, or any other well-meaning organization. Unfortunately, many mothers today think that if they drop their children off at Sunday School or pray over the meal at Thanksgiving and Christmas, they have done their duty in instilling a godly foundation. However, the primary place where children are to learn about God is not in a private school, a parachurch organization, or even the local church. God has given that responsibility to parents, and it is to take place in the home.

Read Deuteronomy 4:1-10. Focus on verses 9-10.

What command is given in this passage?

What is the word of warning?

How might spiritual instruction in the home guard against this problem?

How is this model of Christian education similar to or different from what you experienced as a child?

How is this model of spiritual formation different from what is practiced in your family right now?

In this passage, God commanded the people to live by the decrees and laws He had set forth. God also warned the people not to forget His laws or His miraculous works, and to teach these principles and accounts to the next generation. Throughout Scripture, God commanded parents to instruct their children in the ways of God (Deut. 6:4-12; Prov. 22:6; Eph. 6:4). God's design has always been for parents to be the primary educators of biblical truth. And as a mother, you have the unique opportunity to impart God's truths to your teen girl. You have the ability to impart a wealth of faith to your daughter. Scripture even gives us an indication of how the spiritual instruction of a family (or the lack thereof) can impact a whole family. In the story below, you'll see how one young boy changed his legacy despite the example that was set forth for him. His behavior provides an example to follow in making a difference in the lives of our daughters.

The Boy Who Became King

Scripture leaves us a record of the kings that ruled over the Israelites. The majority left a legacy of doing "what was evil in the Lord's sight." Occasionally, a king would come along and buck the negative trend by doing "what was right in the Lord's sight." One king in particular, King Josiah, was especially commendable. Josiah became king at the young age of eight and changed the culture and direction of the nation.

Read 2 Kings 22:1-2.

How do these verses describe Josiah?

How long did Josiah reign?

What was unusual about his godly behavior?

Verse 2 notes that "he did what was right in the Lord's sight . . . and did not turn to the right or to the left." Now, I don't know if you've been around a typical bunch of eight-year-old boys lately, but doing "what was right in the Lord's sight" does not come naturally unless Mom is threatening to withdraw Nintendo privileges. In fact, the typical résumé of the average eight-year-old boy might include such noteworthy achievements as the ability to belch to the tune of many songs, completely ruin six new pairs of socks in a two-week period, and make a fort in the backyard that includes cacti from the neighbor's professionally landscaped yard. How do I know this? My son, Hayden, managed to pull off each of the above feats by the tender age of eight. Definitely not "king" material.

Notice that Josiah "did what was right in the Lord's sight" despite his religious heritage. In fact, his father and grandfather had enough dysfunction to make the average guest on "The Jerry Springer Show" look normal. Let's look at his family lineage.

Read 2 Kings 21:19-24.

What was Josiah's father's name?

How does Scripture describe him?

What did he do while king of Israel?

His father, King Amon, did "what was evil in the Lord's sight" (2 Kings 21:20), reigned only two years, and was conspired against by his own officials and assassinated in the palace. Not exactly a great role model for a young king to follow. Maybe that's because King Amon's father set a horrible example as well.

Read 2 Kings 21:1-6,16.

What was Josiah's grandfather's name?

How does Scripture describe him?

What evil practices did this king engage in while on the throne?

Josiah's grandfather, King Manasseh, did "what was evil in the Lord's sight" (2 Kings 21:2), reigned 55 years, and "shed so much innocent blood that he filled Jerusalem with it from one end to another" (2 Kings 21:16). He erected altars to Baal, bowed down and worshiped the starry hosts, sacrificed his son in the fire, practiced sorcery and divination, and consulted mediums and spiritists. Not exactly a positive role model for his grandson, Josiah.

Given the example provided by King Amon and Manasseh, I can't help but wonder if Josiah did what was "right in the Lord's sight" because he had a mother who was committed to raising her children to do "what was right in the Lord's sight." Call it speculation, but someone was steering the boy in the right direction.

In the 8th year of Josiah's reign, when he was approximately 16 years old, Scripture notes that Josiah began to "seek the God of his ancestor David." In the 12th year of his reign, when he was approximately 20 years old, he began to "cleanse Judah and Jerusalem," destroying all the pagan shrines, the Asherah poles, and the carved idols and cast images (2 Chron. 34:3).

Perhaps the most defining moment for Josiah came six years later, in the 18th year of his reign. After purifying the land and the temple, he ordered that repairs begin on the "temple of the Lord his God" (2 Chron. 34:8). One day he sent his secretary, Shaphan, to the temple to inform Hilkiah, the high priest, to pay out the workers who were repairing the temple. While performing this task, Hilkiah informed Shaphan that he had found the Book of the Law in the temple of the Lord. Shaphan returned with the book and read from it in the presence of the king. Keep in mind that up until this point Josiah had no knowledge of the book; he was hearing its contents for the first time. When the book was read, Josiah was faced with the sudden realization that God had previously established a covenant with the Israelite people and had set forth a code of conduct for the people to follow. Upon hearing the contents of the book and coming to terms with the shortfall of the Israelite people in meeting God's terms, Josiah humbled himself, tore his robes, and wept in the presence of the Lord (see 2 Kings 22:19).

Josiah's Response, Our Example

Josiah's response to the hearing of the Book of the Law and his subsequent decision to return to the teachings of the Lord can serve as a model to Christian mothers today who are faced with raising their daughters in an ungodly world. Josiah was faced with the same question the Israelites asked God in Malachi 3:7: "How can we return?" Josiah's response ultimately led the Israelite people back to the paths of God. As we look at his response in more detail, take note as to how Josiah was able to counteract the negative influences of the times and return to God. Before you continue reading, check out 2 Kings 22–23 to get the complete story of Josiah.

1. JOSIAH CRIED OUT TO GOD AND WEPT IN HIS PRESENCE

In spite of the fact that Josiah had sought the God of his ancestor David 10 years prior, purified the land four years after that, and recently had begun repairs to the temple, it became clear with the reading of the Book of the Law that the Israelite people had a long way to go in returning to the paths of God. As mothers, we face a similar situation today in raising godly, virtuous daughters. As someone who has been in the trenches of ministry to preteen and teen girls, I have witnessed firsthand the consequences of a culture absent of virtue and the effect it is having on the younger generation. Our worldly culture is exposing our girls to situations they are not equipped to handle. They are forced to grow up too fast.

Like Josiah, we mothers must acknowledge the evil times and cry out to God for help. As Christians, we find ourselves in a sad and desperate state when it comes to the godless influences of our culture. Though

Christians are the majority in this country, I fear that many have become apathetic concerning the times and many more appear to have adopted the attitude: "If you can't beat 'em, join 'em." Over the last several decades, {21} Christians have become more and more desensitized to our worldly culture. Like the church of Laodicea mentioned in the prophetic Book of Revelation, many Christians are left with a lukewarm faith that is "neither cold nor hot" (Rev. 3:15).

When we mothers humble ourselves before God and weep before Him, crying out for direction, God will have mercy and hear our prayers. If you have never been able to weep in the presence of God over the evil in this world, make a point to ask God specifically in your prayer time to break your heart. Like Josiah, our first step is to turn to God for solutions.

Take some time right now to humble yourself before God. Meditate on 2 Chronicles 7:14. If you like to write, use the space provided below to write out a prayer to God. Be honest, vulnerable, and open before God, who already knows your heart. Ask Him for direction in leading your daughter in godliness.

---

2. JOSIAH PLEDGED HIMSELF TO THE COVENANT

The second step Josiah took after discovering the Book of the Law was to gather the people together, from the least to the greatest, and read the entire Book of the Covenant in the hearing of the people. After doing so, he set an example before the people by making a personal pledge before God to wholeheartedly follow the commands set forth in the book: "The king stood by the pillar and made a covenant in the presence of the Lord to follow the Lord and keep His commandments, His decrees, and His statutes with all his mind and with all his heart, and to carry out the words of the covenant that were written in this book; all the people agreed to the covenant" (2 Kings 23:3).

When Christ came, He established a new covenant that set people free from the penalty of the law and instead promised salvation by grace to those who believed on His name. However, it was never God's intent that we ignore the code of conduct He had prescribed. The Bible, combining both the Old and New Covenants, was intended to be everyone's instruction manual for living. In a culture where the majority of the people base moral decisions on "whatever feels right at the time," it has never been more important than now for Christians to pledge themselves and their children to the standards of the Bible.

> *When we devote ourselves to the teachings of God's Word, the Bible becomes our parenting manual. Mothers who choose not to parent by God's Word have by default abdicated the raising of their children to the culture at large.*

It will be impossible to take a stand against the negative influences facing our daughters unless we as mothers are committed to following God and adhering to His commands, regulations, and decrees with all our heart and all our soul, just as Josiah did. When we devote ourselves to the teachings of God's Word, the Bible becomes our parenting manual. Mothers who choose not to parent by God's Word have by default abdicated the raising of their children to the culture at large.

Many of the standard mother-daughter battles are decided in advance when mothers adhere to the standards of God's Word. Christian mothers who choose a position contrary to the standards in God's Word will send a mixed message to their daughters, implying that God's Word is not always relevant in today's world. Children who grow up with compromised standards often believe that rules (even God's rules) were meant to be broken.

Unlike in the days of King Josiah's reign, the Book of the Law has not been lost. Most likely it sits on bookshelves and nightstands in the majority of homes in America. It is the number one best-selling book of all times. Why then are we experiencing a culture that is all but devoid of its teachings and standards? I believe it is due to the fact that so few of Christ's followers have pledged themselves to follow the teachings of Scripture. Though Jesus came to establish a new covenant to supersede the old covenant, He also made clear that He did not come to "destroy the Law or the Prophets" (Matt. 5:17). And while it is important that we not get so carried away with following the letter of the law that we lose sight of grace, it is also important that we not take advantage of God's grace to the extent that we ignore the law.

The Bible is humanity's moral compass, clearly defining good from evil, right from wrong. It is divinely inspired by God. It contains the one "absolute truth" in this world—Jesus Christ. It will be impossible to counteract the negative influences of our culture unless we use the truths set forth in the Bible as our standard. As mothers, we are called to protect our children from anything that would contradict God's truths and standards. Like Josiah, we must pledge ourselves to the Book of the Covenant and become intimately acquainted with its teachings.

Here's a practical example. A friend recently relayed a story about a girl in her church who had become pregnant. Her parents became enraged at the situation and pushed for the girl to get an abortion. Her mother stated, "We don't believe in abortion, but it's the right thing to do." Without knowing it, this girl's parents had taught the girl that God's standards set forth in Scripture don't matter in real life.

Think about your own life and example. How have you taught your daughter that God's Word is the standard for your behavior? On the other hand, can you name some times in which your example taught her that God's Word didn't apply to everyday life? (For example, if you didn't want to talk to someone on the phone, did you tell your daughter to lie and say you weren't at home?) Take some time to jot down some instances. Be honest.

_____

_____

_____

_____

_____

_____

3. JOSIAH TOOK ACTION

Josiah read the Book of the Law in the hearing of the people and pledged to follow the Lord and keep His commands, regulations, and decrees with all his heart and all his soul; but he didn't stop there. The next 17 verses in 2 Kings 23:4-20 detail steps Josiah took to purge the land of evil influences. He removed from the temple all the articles made for Baal or Asherah and burned them in the fields outside Jerusalem. He tore down the quarters of the male prostitutes who were in the temple of the Lord and removed the horses from the entrance of the temple that had been dedicated to the sun. He tore down the pagan altars built by his grandfather, Manasseh, and smashed them to pieces and threw the rubble into the Kidron Valley. In the town of Samaria, he removed and defiled all the shrines the kings of Israel had built that had provoked the Lord to anger.

After Josiah purged the land of its evil influences, he ordered the people to celebrate the Passover as was written in the Book of the Covenant. In 2 Kings 23:25, Josiah was remembered with this legacy: "Before him there was no king like him who turned to the Lord with all his mind and with all his heart and with all his strength according to all the law of Moses, and no one like him arose after him."

Before you jump to conclusions and think I am suggesting that you grab a Bic® lighter and torch everything in sight that promotes evil, hang in there. Remember, Josiah was king and had the power to remove evil influences from the land. Yet even though we do not have the power of a king, there are things we can do to take a stand against negative influences affecting our daughters. And they are legal! Besides, I don't know what is more frightening: an angry king or an angry mob of mothers who are fed up with half-naked divas, sex-laden television shows, and thong underwear marketed to little girls. Watch out world, here we come!

It's time for the silent majority to speak up. It's time to get off the sidelines and enter the battle. It's time for mothers to give it everything they've got. The powerful influences that reign in our culture have taken advantage of the silence. They have grossly underestimated the power of a united front of angry mothers. Mothers are a sleeping giant, and when the giant awakens, take cover—things are going to change! I believe the giant is slowly stirring and beginning to wipe the sleep from its eyes.

Gone are the days when Christian mothers could assume that good would prevail in the land. The Judeo-Christian value system our nation was founded upon has been replaced with secular humanism run amuck. The current intolerance to Christianity has driven many faithful mothers to their knees in battle. While many battles are won as a result of prayer, the battle against the negative influences in our culture will also require action. When Moses and the Israelite people were fleeing Egypt and were hemmed in at the Red Sea with the Egyptians fast approaching on their heels, Moses told the people to be still and watch the deliverance of the Lord. God's response is found in Exodus 14:15: "Why are you crying out to me? Tell the Israelites to break camp." It's time for Christians to break camp.

It is not enough to raise our daughters to be prayer warriors. It is not enough to raise our daughters to be lovers of God's Word. In today's world, we must also raise our daughters to be activists. First, we will have to become activists ourselves. When we mothers find our voice and speak up and then further train our daughters to speak up, we will see positive change. As long as we remain silent, the downturn in morality will continue.

What hinders you from taking direct action on behalf of your daughter?

What action have you seen other mothers take? How did that encourage or discourage you?

Can you think of a time when you boldly took a stand against a negative influence in your daughter's life? If so, describe it.

Think about the actions you need to take in your community, state, or even your own home as an outcry against the negative influences that are shaping the heart of your daughter. Read the following statements and place a check by the ones you will be willing to do in order to take action

for your daughter's sake. Some will apply to your situations. Others will not. If you are new to this commitment to impact your daughter's life and aren't sure you can make any changes just yet, mark the ones you will begin to pray seriously about taking action.

☐ Reducing the channels you subscribe to on cable or satellite, or placing channel blockers on inappropriate networks

☐ Purchasing monitoring and/or filtering software for the computers in your home (Example: E'blaster program from www.spectorsoft.com to monitor incoming and outgoing instant messages and e-mails.

☐ Replacing your daughter's subscriptions to fashion magazines (or your own!) with other reading materials, and then writing a letter to the magazine explaining why you are cancelling the subscription

☐ Contacting the managers at the clothing stores where your daughter shops most frequently, requesting that their company provide more modest alternatives

☐ Running for a place on the school board so that you can have a voice in the curriculum taught in your daughter's school

☐ Other actions you've seen taken _____

Yet to Come

In the next six chapters, we'll take a look at six battles your teenage girl faces: conformity, self-esteem, purity, modesty, boys, and girl politics. Your daughter needs your guidance—your voice—as she navigates these potential land mines in her journey through adolescence. You can play a major role growing your daughter into a godly woman, but you must choose to take an active role in her spiritual development. Remember, you will leave an imprint on the life of your daughter. You must determine what kind of imprint you will leave. Choose wisely, for your daughter's future depends in part on your commitment to leave a godly fingerprint on her life.

1. Henry G. Bosch, "Mother's Influence," *Our Daily Bread*, 27 April 1996.

TALKING POINTS

1. If your daughter is doing the study *His Girl: A Bible Study for Teen Girls* while you are completing this study, she and her group discussed the things in her life that stress her out, including the six battles that will be highlighted in this book (and in her study): conformity, self-esteem, purity, modesty, boys, and girl politics. Ask your daughter which of these issues causes the most stress for her on a daily basis. Ask her to explain why the issues cause her stress. Then share with her the issues that most stressed you out at her age and why they were stressful.

2. Ask your daughter what influences her decision-making most: her family, friends, or the media (music, television, movies, magazines).

3. As a family devotional time, read 2 Chronicles 22–23 (you may need to read this over several days). As a family, discuss the following:
   a. What do you think influenced Josiah to turn back to the Lord?
   b. What kinds of things did Josiah do to show his reverence for God?
   c. Why did Josiah tear his robes?
   d. Why do you think Josiah wept before God?
   e. How can our family more faithfully honor God's Word?
   f. What habits might we as a family need to change in order to honor God's Word? (turn off the TV, pray together, check in on our neighbor more often, and so forth)

4. Relay a time recently when you were tempted to listen to culture's viewpoint instead of God's. Begin by saying something like, "You know, something interesting happened to me the other day, and I want to tell you about it."

5. End your discussion time by asking your daughter how you can be praying for her the following week (upcoming tests, cheer tryouts, conflicts with friends, etc.).

A Mother's Journal

A Mother's Journal

CHAPTER 2

Anticonformity

A S A PARENT VOLUNTEER at my son's high school, I recently attended a meeting of about three hundred students. The meeting was for a student leadership organization that was given the task of voting for the homecoming theme. I watched with interest as students were given four choices for the theme and then asked to raise their hands when their favorite theme was called. I watched a group of about eight to 10 girls as they discussed among themselves which theme they would choose. When it came time for the vote and their preferred selection was called, they raised their hands in unison. As they glanced around the room, it quickly became apparent that their choice was not the popular choice. A few of the girls became visibly uncomfortable and quickly lowered their hands before their vote was counted. I turned to a fellow parent volunteer and said, "Bless their hearts. If they buckle so easily to peer pressure when it comes to the homecoming theme, they don't stand a chance when it comes to drinking, trying drugs, or having sex."

> *I want to raise my children to abide by God's absolute standards consistently and with permanence. Our world is in desperate need of people who will be willing to stand against the culture instead of being shaped by it.*

The next five chapters of this study will deal with specific godly attributes that are contingent on the truths set forth in this chapter. Honestly, it will be difficult to impart the next five godly attributes to your daughter if you and/or she have already conformed to the current culture and the popular opinions of the day. I want to raise my children to abide by God's absolute standards consistently and with permanence. Our world is in desperate need of people who will be willing to stand against the culture instead of being shaped by it.

How have you seen your daughter seek to conform to culture?

How are her struggles to conform to culture like or different from your own struggles to conform to culture when you were a teenager?

Are there times in your life now when you have a tendency to conform to culture? If so, give an example.

Standing Alone

I want my children to be among the remnant of Christians who will stand for God and His standards, even if it means standing alone; and I hope that is your desire for your daughter as well. It is our job as parents to help equip our daughters for that task. However, before we can challenge our girls to be in the world but not live like it, you and I must evaluate whether we're setting a good example in our own lives.

Read 1 Peter 2:9-12.

List below the adjectives in this passage that describe believers. Circle the adjective that best describes you.

Why are believers called a chosen race?

What is the darkness described in verse 9?

According to verse 10, what have you and I received as believers? What difference should that make in our daily lives?

What adjectives did Peter use in verse 11 to describe his readers? Why do you think Peter used those adjectives?

What is the result of living like aliens and strangers in this world?

X   Peter wrote this book to the people of God who had been scattered throughout Asia Minor and the rest of the world. Several times in this letter, he encouraged believers to stand firm in the midst of the persecution they were enduring (1 Pet. 1:6-7; 4:16). It must have been tempting to these believers to conform to the culture. If given the choice between renouncing their faith or being fed to a bunch of hungry lions, they must have wrestled with whether they could just blend in with the culture while maintaining their loyalty to their Savior. Unfortunately, our daughters face the same choice. While they may not be physically persecuted, they do face a culture that demands that they renounce their loyalty to God.

God's Prized Possession

Peter described his readers as "a chosen race, a royal priesthood, a holy nation" and people who had "received mercy" (1 Pet. 2:9-10). These all emphasize God's loving initiative in bringing His people to Himself and allowing us to be a part of His work in the world. It also emphasizes God's ownership in our lives. He has "staked His claim" on our lives. What an amazing thought: we are God's prized possession. We are what His heart desires.

As God's chosen people, we're called to declare His praises. And that shouldn't be difficult once we understand what He's rescued us from. Verse 9 tells us that He's pulled us from darkness into light. Obviously, Peter was using a metaphor here. Darkness and light in the Bible often describe the state of sinfulness versus the state of forgiveness or redemption.

How do you feel knowing that you are God's prized possession? Check any that might apply:

☐ humbled   ☐ embarrassed   ☐ scared   ☐ apathetic

☐ energized   ☐ overwhelmed   ☐ ambiguous   ☐ ashamed

☐ unsure   ☐ overjoyed   ☐ worthless   ☐ unworthy

☐ perplexed   ☐ content   ☐ peaceful   ☐ elated

☐ unsettled   ☐ awed   ☐ confident   ☐ confused

Does knowing how God feels about you change the way you feel about yourself? Why or why not?

Does knowing how God feels about you change the way you want to raise your daughter? Why or why not?

Because of His Mercy

Even more awesome than knowing we are God's prized possession is knowing how we obtain that status. Peter explained that we become God's children simply because of His mercy. The people to whom Peter wrote had lived without God's mercy for a long time. They had tried to earn God's favor and appease His wrath. In the coming of Christ, however, these people experienced mercy in a tangible form.

We live in a culture today that demands we work for our wages. We live in the wealthiest country in the world and applaud those people who earn their keep, make their own way, forge their own path, and "make something of themselves." Unfortunately, that do-it-yourself mentality has crept its way into our understanding of God. We think that we can earn our way to God by our efforts, our money, or our good deeds toward others. Scripture makes clear, however, that one thing we can never earn, despite how much we work, is God's love. It's not for sale at any price. Why? Because it is a gift.

Romans 6:23 says that "The wages of sin is death, but the gift of God is eternal life in Christ Jesus our Lord." This short verse communicates an amazing truth. You and I deserve death—eternal separation from God— { 35 } but God offers us life through His Son, Jesus Christ. This verse doesn't mention going to church, giving money, repeating a prayer, offering a sacrifice, paying penance, or jumping through hoops. His love is unconditional and unmerited. His love was made tangible when He wrapped Himself in human flesh and died on a cross in our place—a demonstration of love beyond comprehension.

He has offered His love and devotion. He longs for us to respond by loving Him in return, but He will not stop loving us even if we choose to reject Him. Those few who choose to respond to His love in repentance and faith will receive all He has to offer—eternal life, hope, and joy.

Maybe you're hearing words of grace for the first time. You've lived under the assumption that you had to please God in order to receive His love. You've jumped through all the hoops of religion and piety, and they've left you longing for something—mercy and grace. Or maybe you once dove deeply into the sea of His love but recently have been living in the shallows.

Take a few moments to write down your response to God for His passionate, unrelenting, faithful, demonstrative love for you shown in tangible form in the sacrifice of Christ.

_____

_____

_____

_____

_____

Daniel: A Man Who Lived as a Stranger

If you've been in church a fair amount of time, you've probably heard about Daniel. As a young man, he stood firm in his convictions against eating the king's food and drinking the king's wine; and God gave him knowledge, understanding, and the ability to understand visions and dreams (Dan. 1:3-20). Let's look a little more closely at this particular story.

Read Daniel 6:1-4.

What did King Darius decide to do?

Why did the king appoint Daniel?

How did Daniel fare in his new responsibilities?

Let's review. Daniel was an Israelite. However, when Nebuchadnezzar conquered Israel, Daniel was taken from Judah to Babylon, where as a young man, he was trained in the language and literature of the Babylonians so he could serve in the king's palace. While he lived in a pagan country, he remained faithful to his God, and God blessed him. When Darius became king, he decided to appoint satraps over his kingdom. The word satrap literally means "protector of the kingdom." These local leaders, comparable to governors, would be responsible for the political affairs of the area granted to them; and each satrap in turn would be held accountable to three administrators who would guard against fraud. They watched over the tax money to ensure that it was properly collected and that these satraps didn't steal from the king—checks and balances. Darius appointed Daniel as one of these high-ranking administrators; and because Daniel distinguished himself above everyone else, the king had planned to promote him above everyone else.

Can you hear the outcry of the Babylonians? This foreigner who had been banished to their country had been promoted to a high position of authority above them. When the satraps and other administrators heard about Darius' plan to promote Daniel, they were outraged.

Read Daniel 6:5-9.

How did the satraps and administrators respond to the news of Daniel's upcoming promotion?

While Daniel didn't hide his faith, many of us living in today's world try to segregate the secular from the sacred. We don't want anyone to know about our faith, so we hide it.

What was the snag in their plans?

How did they finally decide they could trap Daniel?

How did the satraps know this plan would cause a problem for Daniel?

These officials were not too happy at the prospect of Daniel's being promoted above them (translation: they were really jealous), so they tried to discredit him by exposing corruption he had committed. In all likelihood, not all 120 satraps were involved in the plot against Daniel, but it seems likely that both of the other administrators were a part of the coup. The problem was that Daniel was completely trustworthy and free of corruption. Scripture indicates that he was neither dishonest nor negligent in his duties.

Because Daniel's character was above reproach, the officials decided to create a conflict between the government and Daniel's faith. Because Daniel served God alone, they planned to trap him by forcing him to bow down and worship other gods. Daniel would be left with a choice: either follow God or obey the king. It is evident by the officials' actions that Daniel's relationship with God was no secret. Daniel had remained faithful and open about his loyalty to Yahweh even in a pagan land. Even this short segment of verses has a challenge for us. While Daniel didn't hide his faith, many of us living in today's world try to segregate the secular from the sacred. We don't want anyone to know about our faith, so we hide it. It is time for Christians to stop living in seclusion and secret and allow their faith to be known.

The officials "went together" to see the king. While some scholars think this signifies a mob mentality, most think the term carries the idea of acting in concert or in harmony. They were one in their conspiracy. Their plan was simple: the king should establish a law that for 30 days anyone who prayed to another god besides King Darius would be thrown into a den of lions. In ancient times prayers to the gods were mediated through priests, so King Darius would become the priestly mediator for this time period. Such a law would have been a test of loyalty to the king. Thus, Darius wasn't setting himself up as a god but rather as a mediator of the people to the gods. Those who didn't show loyalty faced a gruesome fate. The guilty would be thrown into a den of lions where they would be torn to pieces and devoured.

The officials encouraged the king to "establish the edict and sign the document" (Dan. 6:8). The tone of this phrase indicates a hasty decision. These jealous contemporaries of Daniel wanted the king to make a decision immediately before he could think it through or see the motives behind it. Once signed, the law was irrevocable. Even the king himself couldn't change it. Verse 9 indicates that King Darius signed the document. The officials must have thought that Daniel's fate was sealed. He was fodder for the lions. Read on to discover what happened.

Read Daniel 6:10-18.

How did Daniel respond when he learned about the signed document?

Where did Daniel go? What did Daniel do?

How do we know this was the norm for Daniel?

If you had been in Daniel's sandals, how would you have responded? Would you have prayed openly or would you have closed the shutters?

What did the officials discover? What did they do in response?

What was the king's response to the news of Daniel's defiance?

What was the king eventually forced to do?

What parting words did the king give to Daniel?

What was the night of Daniel's "execution" like for Darius?

Can you imagine Daniel's reaction? He probably had no indication that he was about to be set up for a huge fall. Yet, when he learned that the document had been signed, he continued his discipline of prayer and did not hide it. He went to his house and went upstairs. The fact that Daniel's house had an upstairs may indicate high status. The room wasn't an attic like many Western homes. Rather, like many houses in the East, it was a room on the flat roof with latticed windows so the wind could circulate. The fact that Daniel returned to his place of private worship and prayer shows the measure of his courage and conviction. Even an edict from the king would not sway his devotion.

I love it! With the windows opened toward his homeland, he prayed and gave thanks "as he had done before" (v. 10). Some 70 years had passed since chapter 1 when Daniel was abducted from his homeland as a young lad and taken into captivity by the Babylonians. He was now an elderly man faced with a life-or-death situation. Imagine how easy it would have been to try to justify not bowing down to God for just 30 days. He could still pray without bowing. He could pray in his heart without a public demonstration. At a minimum, it would have been tempting at least to close the windows and pray out of the public eye! The fact that he didn't change his routine makes me wonder if he knew others were watching. If so, to compromise his discipline would mean compromising his witness—something Daniel was unwilling to do. Lion's den or no, Daniel didn't give it a second thought. He simply did what had come naturally for him to do after all these years—go before his God. I wonder if Daniel knew others were watching him. He surely knew that someone would see him through the windows.

Think about your own life. When and with whom are you most tempted to compromise your witness? Check the situations below, and record the reasons and situations in which you are tempted to compromise:

_____ coworker   **Reason or situation:** _____

_____ spouse   **Reason or situation:** _____

_____ relative   **Reason or situation:** _____

_____ church member   **Reason or situation:** _____

_____ neighbor   **Reason or situation:** _____

_____ another parent   **Reason or situation:** _____

_____ close friend   **Reason or situation:** _____

Despite the consequences, Daniel bowed and prayed toward Jerusalem, probably a practice based on Solomon's instructions (see 1 Kings 8:35,38,44,48). Solomon's temple had been in Jerusalem, and the temple had symbolized the presence of God. When Daniel followed through on his act of devotion just as he had done before, his conspirators were waiting in the wings to catch him in their trap. Before long they saw what they had expected—Daniel "petitioning and imploring his God" (v. 11). Daniel's asking for help may imply that Daniel was praying for deliverance from the king's decree or for strength to be faithful. However, the phrase literally means "to show favor or grace," so it seems Daniel was simply asking for God's mercy and grace in his life just as he always had, unmoved by the probable consequences of his actions. He refused to be molded by the pagan culture around him, even if it meant certain death.

Like little children tattling on someone, the satraps and administrators ran to tell on Daniel. Notice verse 13. "Then they replied to the king, 'Daniel, one of the Judean exiles, has ignored you, the king, and the edict you signed, for he prays three times a day'" (Dan. 6:13). Can you hear the jealousy and contempt in their voices? Not only were these men trying to remove Daniel from power, but they were also trying to mock and ridicule him in the process, making him seem more disloyal to the king. They explained that Daniel had ignored the king, meaning that Daniel didn't think the king was important. Further, Daniel didn't pay attention to the king's edict, demonstrating his disloyalty. In fact, so great was Daniel's disloyalty that he disobeyed the king three times a day. What king wouldn't be enraged at such defiance?

The king was indeed grieved, but not for the reasons the officials had envisioned. Scripture indicates that the king was "very displeased" (v. 14). Darius was not upset because Daniel had been praying (as the king's actions later show) but because he saw for the first time the real reason for the decree. He had been manipulated and deceived and was distressed at Daniel's situation. He desperately wanted to save Daniel from the decree and was set on trying to rescue him. He worked until sundown, which means the law was probably written so that the punishment would be carried out the same day as the crime. At the end of the day, the conspirators reminded the king of his decree and waited for the king to make good on his word.

Because the decree couldn't be overturned, the king gave the order. Daniel was arrested and thrown into the lion's den to await a horrible end. Darius's concern is touching. He said, "May your God, whom you serve continually, rescue you!" (v. 16). A stone was placed over the opening of the den, and the king sealed Daniel's doom with his own signet ring so that no one would dare attempt to rescue Daniel. Knowing the gravity of the situation and his own role in Daniel's demise, the king went back to the palace and spend the night fasting. He refused any kind of entertainment, and he could not sleep. So how does the story end?

Read Daniel 6:19-24.

Who went to the lion's den first?

When did he go? What might this tell you about him and his situation?

What did he ask? Why do you think he asked such a question?

What did Daniel say? What was the king's response to God?

What happened to the satraps and administrators who had conspired against Daniel?

In ancient Babylonia, a tortured victim would be pardoned if he or she had not died by the following day. This practice was probably still in play when the king went to find Daniel. When he reached the den, he "cried out in anguish" (v. 20) to Daniel. He held out hope that Daniel might be alive, but his anguish showed that this hope was dim. The king acknowledged the God Daniel served, but he didn't necessarily believe in Yahweh's power.

Adjectives fail to describe how Darius must have felt to hear Daniel's voice bellow from the depths of the cave: delight, astonishment, relief, awe, disbelief, joy. Daniel said, "My God sent His angel and shut the lions' mouths" (v. 22). Notice who received the credit. His God. He explained that God had sent an angel to protect him against the lions because he had committed no crime against the king—he was innocent. In fact, the angel had prevented him from being harmed in any way. Apparently, the lions' deadly teeth and claws were incapacitated.

The king was "overjoyed" at the amazing turn of events and ordered that Daniel be taken out of the den. From the depths of the cave he surfaced unscathed, unscarred, and unmarred. The reason for this miracle? "He trusted in his God" (v. 23). But the story doesn't end there. God had vindicated Daniel before the king. That left the conspiring satraps and administrators. King Darius called for the men who had "maliciously accused" (v. 24) Daniel. This phrase literally translates as "who had eaten his pieces." These same men who had "eaten pieces" of Daniel (spoken maliciously against him) would soon be eaten themselves—literally. These men were thrown into the lions' den along with their wives and children (preventing any retaliation from family members). Lest anyone think these lions were too old, weak, or fat to devour anyone, the Scripture tells us that the lions pounced on these wicked officials before they had even reached the bottom of the lions' den.

The Rest of the Story

The king issued a decree ordering all people to give reverence to the God of Daniel. In fact, Darius declared that "He is the living God and He endures forever; His kingdom will never be destroyed, and His dominion has no end. He rescues and delivers; He performs signs and wonders in the heavens and on the earth, for He has rescued Daniel from the power of the lions" (vv. 26-27). A god who performed the miracles Darius had seen was indeed worthy of worship and reverence. How ironic that a pagan king in a pagan land would declare such truth about Yahweh God. God indeed received the glory due His name. Scripture goes on to say that Daniel prospered during the time of Darius. The plot had indeed been foiled, for Daniel was promoted after all!

Reflecting on Daniel's Story

If we desire to raise daughters who, like Daniel, do not conform to the "standards" of our culture, we mothers must also refuse to conform. Like Daniel, we must serve our God "continually" (v. 16). The Hebrew word for "continually" is *tediyra,* which in its original sense means "enduring, permanence, or constantly." Do you live according to God's Word consistently and with permanence; or does your commitment fluctuate such that you, at times, conform to the culture at large? What about your daughter(s)?

Take a moment to reflect on your life and on your daughter's life. On a scale from 1-10, 1 being totally comfortable in this culture, how much of an alien do you think you are? Chart your answers. Be honest!

In what areas are you too comfortable in this world?

_____

_____

_____

_____

Now, put yourself in your daughter's shoes for a minute. How would she rank you? Indicate it below.

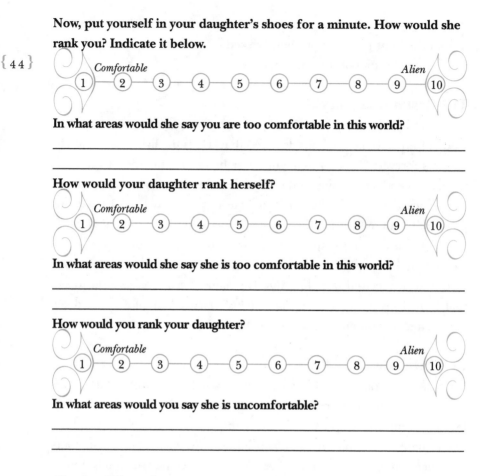

Comfortable — 1 — 2 — 3 — 4 — 5 — 6 — 7 — 8 — 9 — 10 — Alien

In what areas would she say you are too comfortable in this world?

_____

_____

How would your daughter rank herself?

Comfortable — 1 — 2 — 3 — 4 — 5 — 6 — 7 — 8 — 9 — 10 — Alien

In what areas would she say she is too comfortable in this world?

_____

_____

How would you rank your daughter?

Comfortable — 1 — 2 — 3 — 4 — 5 — 6 — 7 — 8 — 9 — 10 — Alien

In what areas would you say she is uncomfortable?

_____

_____

Closing Thoughts

You may have come to the sobering realization that you and/or your daughter(s) have conformed to the culture. Don't be discouraged. It's never too late to get back on track. It will take hard work and effort, but it will be well worth it. Talk to your daughter. Humbly and honestly confess to her (and God) your sin of conformity and share your heart's desire to change. If she is in middle school or older and has grown accustomed to loose boundaries regarding the influences of the culture, you can count on resistance. The older she is, the more attached she will be to the world. New boundaries will need to be set to protect her from the influences of the culture and further temptation to conform to it. Remember, you are called to be her mother first and then her friend!

TALKING POINTS

1. Tell your daughter about a time as a teenager when you chose to go against the crowd. If you were typically a conformist, tell her about times you wish you would have taken a stand and not conformed.

2. Share with your daughter an area in your life right now where you're tempted to conform to the world. Encourage her to share one area in her life. Stop and pray together about those areas of temptation.

3. As a family (husband and other children included), evaluate areas in which your family may be conforming to the world. Think about the following areas: movies you buy or rent, living beyond your financial means in order to keep up with everyone else, going to a particular church in order to be recognized, watching TV programs even though the themes are blatantly ungodly, or spending too much time with people who negatively influence you to conform to the culture.

4. The next time you watch a movie or TV show together, stop and talk about how that program (and especially the commercials) tries to entice you both to be like the world.

5. Together, read a biography of a person whom your daughter admires. Discuss ways this person has conformed to the culture as well as ways he or she has chosen to go against the grain.

A Mother's Journal

A Mother's Journal

CHAPTER 3

The Secret of Self-Worth

KATIE IS THE GIRL NEXT DOOR. She is pretty, gets good grades, was voted "Most Popular" by her junior class last year, and went on an overseas mission trip with her youth group. Her peers come to her with their problems. She has a great-looking boyfriend, and she drives a nice (but not fancy) car to school. She's also miserable. She constantly fears that she'll gain weight; she wonders if her friends really like her or if they just like being around her because she's in the "in" crowd; she thinks she's a failure if she makes a bad grade and worries that her boyfriend will break up with her if she won't have sex with him. At times, the pressure to have the perfect body, to be the perfect student, the perfect friend, and the perfect girlfriend overwhelms her. When the stress gets too intense, she takes the edge off by cutting herself. Nobody notices, though, because she has become a master at hiding her secret shame. She locks the door to her bedroom, closes the blinds, plays her favorite CD, and uses a razor blade to make superficial marks across parts of her body most easily hidden.

The need to feel important, valued, and loved is a drive everyone feels; but it is heightened in adolescence. The changes a teenager experiences emotionally, physically, hormonally, and cognitively often leave teens confused about who they are and why they matter.

To her, it's a form of release when the pressure for perfection becomes too much. After it's over, she says she feels "cleansed, calm, in control."

While most teen girls deal with the struggles with self-worth in a different way from Katie, the pressure is still intense. The need to feel important, valued, and loved is a drive everyone feels; but it is heightened in adolescence. The changes a teenager experiences emotionally, physically, hormonally, and cognitively often leave teens confused about who they are and why they matter. As a mother, one of the greatest gifts you can give your daughter is the secret to obtaining true self-worth. Like Katie, your daughter needs to learn a solid basis for her self-worth that is independent of how she looks, what she does, or what others think. Unfortunately, many mothers are unable to give their daughters something that they themselves have yet to discover.

This chapter may be a difficult one for you to dive into because you struggle with your sense of worth. Don't shy away from the truths in this chapter because they can be transformational. And don't feel like you're the only one who struggles with worth and value. If you were to poll a random sampling of mothers of teens, you'd find a vast majority of them still wrestle with their worth. We've all been conditioned by the world to base our worth on external factors, but those foundations will crumble. The only way you and I will ever find true self-worth is in what God believes about us. But before we discover what God thinks of us, we'll review the world's negative and faulty formulas of self-worth.

Faulty Formula 1: Worth = Appearance

This formula is simple. If you look great on the outside, then you're worth something. If you're physically attractive, doors will open for you, people will listen to you, and you will succeed in life. If this is a faulty formula you've been duped into believing, you're not alone. This formula has been around for centuries. Even a prophet of God got it wrong.

Read 1 Samuel 16:1-13.

Who is God's prophet in this story?

What did God command him to do? (v. 1)

How would he know whom to anoint as the new king?

Whom did Samuel initially think God would anoint as king? Why?

What was God's admonition to Samuel?

Who was eventually anointed as the king and Saul's successor?

What was so unusual about this choice?

How does Scripture describe David?

Does it seem surprising to you that God would choose David since He had already told Samuel that He looks on the heart and not the outward appearance? Why or why not?

In this story God had already rejected Saul as the king of Israel. He charged Samuel with the task of anointing a new king from the house of Jesse. Although Samuel was afraid of Saul's retaliation (who wouldn't be), Samuel followed God's command and went to Bethlehem. Once there he went to the house of Jesse and instructed the family to follow the rituals for cleansing prior to a sacrifice. When Jesse and his sons arrived at the prescribed location for the sacrifice, Samuel took one look at Eliab, Jesse's firstborn son, and was impressed at his height and appearance. He wrongly assumed that Eliab would be the next king. After all, the previous king he had anointed was "a head taller than any of the others" (1 Sam. 10:23).

Before Samuel could break out the oil for anointing, God stopped him in his tracks. He hadn't chosen Eliab. He explained to Samuel that "man does not see what the Lord sees, for man sees what is visible, but the Lord sees the heart" (1 Sam. 16:7). The Message paraphrases this verse by stating, "God judges persons differently than humans do. Men and women look at the face; God looks into the heart." Samuel missed it. God wasn't looking for good looks. He was looking for a good heart. In fact, in choosing David, He chose a man after God's own heart (Acts 13:22).

David was described as having "beautiful eyes and a healthy, handsome appearance" (v. 12) These physical features were no proof of his value, for God had already rejected a prime candidate in the handsome category. What mattered was the young boy's heart, which only God could discern. This story also teaches us that having a good physical appearance isn't inherently wrong, but using external appearance as a measure of worth is definitely faulty.

Can you think of a time when you wrongly assessed a person's value based on what he or she looked like? If so, jot it down here.

Have you ever been wrongly judged because of your physical appearance? How did that feel?

Have you ever struggled with feeling like you weren't valued or loved because of your physical appearance? In what situations do you struggle most with basing your worth on what you look like?

Time for Honesty

If we're honest, we have probably all been guilty to some degree of buying into the lie that "worth = appearance." And unknowingly, we've passed on that formula to our daughters. For example, mothers who obsess over their weight, body shape, or appearance in general and complain in the hearing of their daughters send a message that supports that formula. What message are you sending to your daughter if you're always on a diet, worry about gaining weight, obsess about "looking good," and talk about how bad you look? The message is clear and wrong.

Even if a mother has modeled properly defined worth to her daughter, {53} she will be unable to completely shield her from the world's influence. The formula "worth = appearance" has saturated our culture and captured the minds of our daughters. Young girls say that they are more afraid of being fat than they are of cancer, nuclear war, or losing their parents.[1] Is it surprising that the number-one wish for girls aged 11 to 17 is to be thinner?[2] Our daughters are under tremendous pressure to conform their appearance to the unrealistic ideal created by the culture. Girls who measure themselves against the standard imposed by the culture will quickly become dissatisfied. If our daughters are not raised to understand the true formula for self-worth, they will almost certainly grow up and join the ranks of countless women who forever grumble at their reflection in the mirror.

Mothers who dismiss fashion magazines as harmless entertainment should think twice. Researchers have found that women who looked at ads featuring stereotypically thin and beautiful women showed more signs of depression and were more dissatisfied with their bodies after only one to three minutes of viewing the pictures.[3] Our culture esteems beautiful women with perfect bodies. *Sports Illustrated* knows an annual "personality issue" won't sell magazines, but a "swimsuit issue" will. From the time our daughters are young, the world's formula of "worth = appearance" has permeated their minds through fairy tales with beautiful princesses, fashion dolls with figures that are unrealistic, and magazines touting the latest beauty secrets. Our daughters are left with the clear implication that beauty is the ticket to happiness and fulfillment. If Marilyn Monroe were still alive, she might attest otherwise. The numerous media accounts of beautiful celebrities and supermodels frequenting rehab clinics might also suggest that beauty isn't the answer to true self-worth.

Teaching daughters how to dress fashionably, apply appropriate makeup, and coordinate styles of clothes is a valid pursuit for mothers and daughters. Daughters don't automatically know what looks best on them or what matches. However, it is destructive to create a situation in which daughters feel they must measure up to their mother's standard of fashion and beauty.

Breaking free from this faulty formula of self-worth takes courage. Could you stand in front of a full-length mirror while wearing your swimsuit and say, "I am fearfully and wonderfully made"? Many of you just cringed at the thought, which indicates how much this faulty formula of self-worth has permeated your thinking. If you're still struggling with this lie, there's a good chance your daughter will struggle with it as well.

Faulty Formula 2: Worth = What You Do

Unfortunately, most adults have bought into the world's formula that "worth = what you do," so they naturally pass on the dangerous lie to their children. In fact, before I came to depend on God's formula for worth, I modeled "worth = what you do" to my daughter. When my daughter, Paige, was two years old, I signed us up for a mom and tot gymnastics class, hoping it would not only serve as an outlet to expend her boundless energy, but also give us an opportunity to spend time together. My dreams of mother-daughter bonding were dashed on the first day of class when she pushed me aside and said, "I do it myself." (I know you can relate!) I was banished to the sidelines for the remainder of the class. While other mothers and daughters were somersaulting down the mats, my little one kept wandering over to the three- to four-year-old class to do roundoffs and handstands with the big girls. Within weeks the coaches gave in and put her in the older class, thus beginning her gymnastics career. She loved gymnastics, and it was clear from the beginning that she was a natural at the sport. At the age of five, she was invited to be on a show team that performed at local parades and events. The workouts were rigorous because they were grooming these girls for future competition. Of course, as a mother I was proud of my little girl!

However, what had started years before as a form of recreation had progressed to three classes and seven hours a week in the gym at the age of five. Paige loved the costumes, performances, and applause; but she was beginning to show signs of stress from the long workouts. She began crying on the way to class and would tell me she wanted to play with her friends after school. Rather than respond to her cues, I found myself giving her pep talks on the way to class about the importance of persistence and hard work. Not a bad lesson to learn, unless of course, you are five years old and want to come home from kindergarten and just be a kid. Finally, after much soul-searching, I came face-to-face with the realization that I was pushing her in gymnastics for all the wrong reasons. I wanted her to excel with the hopes that it would boost her esteem in future years. My own worth had benefited, albeit temporarily, from my success in gymnastics; and I wanted the same for her. I withdrew her from the class and have never regretted it for a minute. Years later she is casually involved in gymnastics, and her worth is not defined by her success in the sport.

While we should encourage our daughters to strive for excellence and work to the best of their God-given abilities, we need to be careful that we do not send a mixed message that emphasizes achievements as a means to define self-worth.

We have all witnessed parents who attempt to live vicariously through their child so they can selfishly say, "That's my kid." If you don't believe me, just head on out to the nearest Little League field or watch the headlines for stories about parents who beat up other parents over cheerleading tryouts or playing time. Others rationalize, as I had, that pushing their children to succeed provides them with a means to feel worth. This behavior is not exclusive to the ball field or gym. Many Christian parents put far too much emphasis on their children's grades, believing that good grades lead to good colleges, and good colleges lead to good jobs, and good jobs lead to money and success, and money and success ultimately lead to happiness. While we should encourage our daughters to strive for excellence and work to the best of their God-given abilities, we need to be careful that we do not send a mixed message that emphasizes achievements as a means to define self-worth.

Did your parents unknowingly (or purposely) teach you the idiom that your worth is based on performance? If so, in what way?

How have you been guilty of teaching your daughter the formula that "worth = what you do"? In what areas of her life might you be imprinting a faulty message? Check all that apply:

☐ church attendance   ☐ grades

☐ boyfriend   ☐ sports

☐ volunteer work   ☐ family chores

☐ hobbies   ☐ following the crowd

☐ participation in church activities

In what ways have you been guilty of living vicariously through your daughter? In other words, have you derived your own self-worth based on your daughter's successes?

How can you encourage your daughter to pursue excellence in her pursuits without sending the message that worth is obtained by her success?

A survey of teenage girls found that while teenage girls today are more independent and see greater opportunities available to them than their baby boomer parents did at their age, they have less self-confidence and weaker self-images than their parents' generation.[4] Our daughters are craving a worth that cannot be found through numerous achievements. In order to effectively counteract the world's formula of "worth = what you do," we must first make sure we have not fallen prey to believing the formula ourselves. It will be impossible to pass down the true formula for worth to our children unless we have broken free from the lie ourselves.

Faulty Formula 3: Worth = What Others Think of You

Perhaps one of the most commonly uttered phrases by a parent to a teen child is, "You shouldn't care so much about what other people think." When girls are young, they look for approval from their parents. They want praise for the picture they drew in preschool or the castle they built with blocks. As they approach late grade school, they begin to look for approval from their friends. It's not just important that they have friends; they must have a best friend. To be someone's best friend is a validation that says, "I choose you. You win." Unfortunately, any boost to a young girl's sense of worth is often offset by cruel remarks and backbiting among other girls.

As girls discover the ups and downs of adolescence, it's not long before they come to the realization that boys don't have cooties. Before long, the desire for a best friend is replaced with a desire for a boyfriend. Again, to have a boyfriend is a validation of worth. To be chosen is a measure of value, while being left out is a statement as well. (Remember those days of being asked—or not—to go to the prom?)

Whether consciously or not, our daughters learn what actions will gain approval from others. Unfortunately for many girls, winning the approval of others often comes with a heavy price. Girls who have not learned the true formula for worth are easy prey to peer pressures of every sort. As they give in to the desire to please others, it leaves them with a temporary relief that they fit in. The effects, however, are short-term; and "fitting in" to feel worth will leave them feeling worthless in the end. Christian girls are not exempt from seeking worth through others' approval. Surely we can think of Christian adults who have yet to shed their people-pleasing tendencies. At times, I still find myself affected by others' opinions and have to remind myself of the one true formula for worth.

How have you been guilty of living under the faulty formula that your worth is based on what others think of you?

Can you recall a time when you let someone else's approval determine your worth? Think about a coworker, family member, or even your spouse.

What is the problem with allowing another person's opinion to determine your worth?

How have you seen your daughter allow the opinions of others to dictate her worth?

How can you teach your daughter to value the insight and opinions of others without allowing people to determine her worth?

Worth = Who You Are in Jesus Christ

True self-worth can be found only by examining who we are as individuals created by God. While the world defines worth according to appearance, God is more concerned with the heart. While the world's measure of importance is how much you succeed, God has already called you valuable despite what you do. And while most of us struggle with what others think of us, we're the apple of God's eye (Ps. 17:8).

Read Psalm 139:13-14.

In the space below, rewrite these verses in your own words.

What was the psalmist's response to God for creating him?

When was the last time you praised God for creating you as He did? What might that say about how you view yourself?

You've probably read this passage before. You might have told yourself, "Yeah, I've heard this before. I'm made by God, blah, blah, blah." You've become so familiar with the verses that they no longer carry meaning. But think for a minute. The God of the universe—the One who determined where the planets would align, the One who stretched the giraffe's neck and crafted with intricate care the wings on a hummingbird, the One who keeps the earth spinning on its axis—knitted you together like a beautiful tapestry. Those veins you try to cover with makeup and moisturizer were handcrafted by God Almighty. The compassion you show toward others in their deepest pain was designed by Yahweh. Your creative flair and love for people was no mistake. God formed that in your personality. The Master Creator of all that exists also formed you.

The Book of Ephesians also proclaims in poetic form who and what we are as the Beloved of God. Read and meditate upon Ephesians 1:4-8 and jot down your answers to the following questions:

In these verses, what adjectives describe believers?

Which of these adjectives is most significant to you?

According to this passage, what is the basis for God's love and acceptance?

The apostle Paul wrote this letter to the people in Ephesus. In it, he proclaimed the blessings we receive in Christ. We are holy and blameless in His sight (v. 4); we are adopted as His children (v. 5); we are redeemed (bought back) and forgiven (v. 7). In this understanding of standing before God lies the real basis for self-worth. We have worth because God says we have worth. The Message Bible expresses these verses beautifully. It reads:

"Long before he laid down earth's foundations, he had us in mind, had settled on us as the focus of his love, to be made whole and holy by his love. Long, long ago he decided to adopt us into his family through Jesus Christ. (What pleasure he took in planning this!) He wanted us to enter into the celebration of his lavish gift-giving by the hand of His beloved Son. Because of the sacrifice of the Messiah, his blood poured out on the altar of the Cross, we're a free people—free of penalties and punishments chalked up by all our misdeeds. And not just barely free, either. Abundantly free!" (Eph. 1:4-7, *The Message*).

Our goal as mothers should be to raise our daughters to understand that God has "settled on us as the focus of his love, to be whole and holy by his love." We want to raise our daughters to say sincerely, "I will praise You, because I have been remarkably and wonderfully made. Your works are wonderful, and I know this very well" (Ps. 139:14). Of course, they are more likely to respond that way if we can claim the truth for ourselves. It's one thing to acknowledge that you are remarkably and wonderfully made, but do you know it "very well"? Mothers who know it very well stand a greater chance of raising daughters who know it very well. When they come to terms with the awesome realization that they were remarkably and wonderfully made by the Creator of the universe, they will be able to stare at their reflection in the mirror and say, "Beautiful."

Closing Thoughts

At a recent women's event where I was the keynote speaker, I opened my message with this question: "If you could be anyone in the world, who would it be?" I shared that I had a framed picture of the person that I would most like to be. I held the framed picture close to myself so the women were unable to see whose picture was in the frame. I asked three volunteers to come up and, one at a time, take a look at my picture to see if it was the person that had come to their minds. One at a time, I allowed each woman to take a peek at the picture. Each one shook her head back and forth, indicating that the picture in the frame was not the person she had chosen. I then held up the framed picture for all to see. It was a framed mirror. How sad that so few women, if given a choice, would choose to be themselves. I want to raise a daughter who has discovered the one true formula for worth and, as a result, finds contentment in being herself.

1. http://www.ptonthenet.com/articleprint.aspx?ArticleID=1935&m=439.
2. Ibid.
3. Laurie Mintz, lead author of the study and an associate professor of educational and counseling psychology at University of Missouri-Columbia, ABCnews.com, 30 October 2002, http:// www.abcnews.go.com/sections/living/Healthology/HSsupermodel_depressionson021029.html.
4. Survey conducted by the Vagisil Women's Health Center at the annual convention of the American Association for Health Education; 1998.

TALKING POINTS

1. Discuss with your daughter the faulty self-worth formula that ensnares you most often. For example, tell a story of a time when someone else's opinion mattered too much to you.

2. As a family (other siblings and father included), discuss ways in which you as a family may have encouraged faulty self-worth models. You might want to tackle one faulty formula at a time. For example, sit down after dinner and talk about the problems with basing your worth on what you do. Then ask if your daughter feels pressure from you to be perfect. Apologize to your daughter if you've been deriving some self-worth from the success of her activities. This may be a painful experience, but it will be healing as well.

3. Take time with your daughter to read and discuss the following Scriptures that further confirm a biblical self-esteem. Once you've read each of the Scriptures, choose several to memorize together. Reinforce her understanding of these Scriptures by posting them in several places around the house (on the refrigerator, on the bathroom mirror, in her backpack or lunch, and so forth).

Apple of God's Eye—Psalm 17:8
Bought with a Price—1 Cor. 6:20
Chosen by God—1 Peter 2:9
Conqueror—Romans 8:37
God's Workmanship—Eph. 2:10
Inscribed on His Palms—Isa. 49:16
Called by Name—Isaiah 43:1
New Creation—2 Cor. 5:17
No Longer a Slave to Sin—Rom. 6:6
Precious in His Sight—Isaiah 43:4

Belong to God—John 17:9
Child of God—John 1:12
Coheir with Christ—Rom. 8:17
Free from Blemish—Col. 1:22
Loved—Isaiah 43:4
Made by Him—Psalm 100:3
Never Forsaken—Hebrews 13:5
An Overcomer—1 John 5:4-5
Rescued—Colossians 1:13
Royalty—Romans 8:16-17

A Mother's Journal

A Mother's Journal

CHAPTER 4

The Pure Life

ONE OF THE GREATEST CHALLENGES our daughters will face is in regard to sexual purity. In a culture obsessed with sex and steeped in sexual imagery, our daughters are inundated with influences that encourage them to cultivate their sensuality. Sensuality sells shampoo, cars, jeans, undergarments, beer, perfume, CDs, movies, and much more. The sexual revolution initiated in the 1960s, which trivialized sex as nothing more than an extracurricular activity, has succeeded. The rampant sensuality that pervades our society today is a natural by-product of the downgrading in our society of sex from sacred to secular.

Three decades after it began, the sexual revolution that promised women independence and empowerment has, instead, robbed women and girls of their dignity and self-worth. If there is any doubt as to the damage that has resulted from the sexual revolution of the early 1970s, consider that from 1971 to 1979, the percentage of females aged fifteen to nineteen who had had sexual intercourse increased from 30 to 50 percent.[1] From 1978 to 2001, the percentage of high school teens having sex would fluctuate only plus or minus 6 percent.

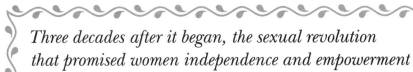

Three decades after it began, the sexual revolution that promised women independence and empowerment has, instead, robbed women and girls of their dignity and self-worth.

While the physical consequences of the sexual revolution clearly are devastating, the emotional consequences are even greater. A recent study links depression and suicide to teen sex. The findings are particularly true for young girls, according to the Heritage Foundation, which sponsored the research. The study found that about 25 percent of sexually active girls say they are depressed all, most, or a lot of the time as compared to 8 percent of girls who are not sexually active. The study also found that 14 percent of girls who have had intercourse have attempted suicide as compared to 6 percent of sexually inactive girls.[2]

Even if your daughter has signed a virginity pledge and you are confident that she is committed to sexual purity, I highly encourage you to set aside time to discuss with her the issue of sexual purity. I recommend that you take your daughter on a weekend getaway specifically to talk about aspects of her purity. I suggest that you incorporate something fun into the weekend to make it something she looks forward to and reflects back on in a positive manner. Most girls are ready to absorb the following information sometime between their seventh- and eighth-grade year in school or around the ages of 12 to 14; however, each girl is different. It is best if you can have the "sex talk" weekend with your daughter before she hears lies about sex elsewhere. The only way our daughters can counteract the lies of our culture regarding sex is for us to give them accurate Bible-based information about sex. Mothers should be the primary source of accurate information.

Reasons Girls Should Wait to Have Sex Until Marriage

In any discussion of sexual purity, mothers should say more than "don't have sex until marriage because I said so." Teens want to understand the reasons behind the principles; arbitrary rules mean nothing to them. We should provide them with clear-cut reasons to abstain from sex until they are married. Following are five reasons girls should wait until marriage to have sex. The first reason alone is reason enough to abstain. However, many Christian girls choose to ignore God's truths and principles regarding right and wrong behavior. They have been taught that sex outside of marriage is wrong, but they have been enticed by the pleasures of the world. Reasons two through five should provide extra ammunition for you in your efforts to raise sexually pure daughters. The reasons are short and to the point.

1. THE OWNERSHIP FACTOR

Every preteen and teen should memorize 1 Corinthians 6:18-20 before they encounter sexual temptation: "Flee from sexual immorality! 'Every sin a person can commit is outside the body,' but the person who is sexually immoral sins against his own body. Do you not know that your body is a sanctuary of the Holy Spirit, who is in you, whom you have from God? You are not your own, for you were bought at a price; therefore glorify God in your body."

Mothers should be purposeful in teaching their daughters that virginity pledges are made to God and that they cover not only sexual intercourse but other sexually impure acts as well. I have spoken with many Christian teens who have justified that "everything but sexual intercourse is OK." One of the most commonly asked questions I receive from teens is, "How far is too far?" I share this answer: "Whatever you would feel uncomfortable doing if Jesus were present—and be assured, He is."

2. THE REGRET FACTOR

Seventy-two percent of teen girls regret their decision to have sex and wish they had waited.[3] While our culture has brainwashed young women into thinking that "empowerment" includes the right to sex with no strings attached, true empowerment is found in saying no to sex before marriage. Additionally, 89 percent of teen girls surveyed in a 2002 study said their peers (teen girls) feel pressure from boys to have sex.[4]

Mothers need to let their daughters know that it is not uncommon for their daughters' friends to attempt to convince them to have sex if they themselves have had sex. Even though most girls regret the decision, it makes them feel they are not alone in their decision. We need to point out to our daughters that it makes no sense to engage in an activity that brings regret to most girls. None of the girls who choose to wait until marriage to have sex report having regrets. The choice is simple: do they want to have regrets or not?

3. THE REPUTATION FACTOR

Ninety-one percent of teens surveyed said a girl can get a bad reputation if she has sex.[5] The double standard still exists today. Girls may think that boys will like them more if they have sex, but in reality boys respect the girls who choose to save sex for marriage. Some things never change. In the same survey, 92 percent of teens said it is generally considered a good thing for a girl to be a virgin.[6]

One teen boy confirmed the above in a letter to an advice columnist: "Dear Abby: I'm a guy, 18, and I have something to say to girls who sleep around. They may think they are 'hot stuff,' but they should hear what is said about them in the locker room. These poor girls think it is flattering to be sought out—that it is a compliment to have sex. Not so! It is cheap and degrading to be used."[7]

4. THE DISEASE FACTOR

One out of four sexually active teens gets a sexually transmitted disease every year.[8] If your daughter is in high school, have her count up her friends who are sexually active. Ask her to divide that number by four. Tell her that is the number of girls who, according to this survey, will become infected with an STD. Some STDs are incurable, and others can hinder or even prevent young women from bearing children. Remind your daughter that out of any given group of teens who practice abstinence, the number who will become infected by an STD is zero.

5. THE PREGNANCY FACTOR

If none of the above reasons is enough to sway a girl from having sex before marriage, perhaps the reality of this one will. A whopping 35 to 40 percent of teen girls will become pregnant at least once by age 20.[9] Therefore, 4 of every 10 teen girls will be faced with the reality of raising a child, placing a child up for adoption, or having an abortion. Regardless of the choice, emotional scars will leave their mark for years to come.

Living by Your Example

Believe it or not, your daughter will take her cues about sexual purity from your example. You may be asking yourself, How can I model sexual purity to my daughter when I'm married? Or, I've already lost my virginity. How can I be a model of purity? Here's the simple answer: Much of the battle over sexual purity takes place outside the bedroom. Purity can be modeled in every aspect of life, and sexual purity can be modeled by both married and single people.

Read 1 Corinthians 6:18-20.

According to this passage, what should believers avoid (flee from)?

What is God's dwelling place? How should this change a person's behavior?

Paul stated that believers were bought at a price. What price was that?

What was Paul's command to believers in verse 20?

What are some ways a believer can honor God with his or her body?

Paul wrote his letter to the believers at Corinth to address several problems the church was facing. The most serious of these issues was being too "Corinthian." The city of Corinth was pagan in both its religious practices and its moral conduct. Corinth was famous for its moral corruption even among other pagan nations. The city was synonymous with actions such as idolatry, adultery, homosexuality, theft, and drunken orgies, just to name a few. Many of these pagan citizens became followers of Christ. However, some continued to live in gross immorality even after their conversion. Like many believers today, these Christians had a rather difficult time not mimicking the world in which they lived. They were conforming to the culture around them, and that culture was ungodly.

In 1 Corinthians 6, Paul turned his attention to a serious problem among these believers—sexual immorality. In verses 12-17, he addressed the problem of sexual union with a prostitute. While this may seem like a no-brainer to you and me, the people of Corinth were struggling with this sinful practice. They lived in a culture in which sexual intercourse with a prostitute was a common occurrence. Many believers had formerly been guilty of such behavior; and like many believers today, they struggled with breaking their ties with their former lifestyles.

Paul's command in verse 18 was simple and straightforward: "flee from sexual immorality!" The verb tense in the Greek could be translated as "flee continually and keep on fleeing until the danger is past." Need a good role model? Think Joseph when confronted by Potiphar's wife. No discussion. No rationalization. No weighing the pros or cons. Run away and keep running.

What are we running from? Sexual immorality. The word in the Greek is *porneia* from which we derive our word *pornography*. In Paul's day, this word encompassed any sexual sin—including but not limited to adultery, homosexuality, and premarital sex. Sounds simple, doesn't it? Flee from sexual sin. You might be tempted to turn off your brain, thinking that this passage doesn't really apply to you since you're faithful to your spouse. Don't be fooled.

Read Psalm 101:3 and Philippians 4:8.

What was the psalmist's promise before God?

What are some examples of vile things people set before their eyes?

What did Paul tell the Philippian believers (and us) to think about? List them in the space below. Then next to them, cite some examples of fallacies or untruths concerning sexual purity that our culture spouts off. An example is provided for you.

Things to Think About	Culture's Thoughts
Things that are true	It's OK to have sex if you love the person.

Psalm 101:3 says, "I will not set anything godless before my eyes." Other translations say: "I will set no worthless thing before my eyes" (NASB). "I will refuse to look at anything vile and vulgar" (NLT). "I will set before my eyes no vile thing" (NIV). "I will not look at anything wicked" (NCV). The Message paraphrases this verse as, "I refuse to take a second look at corrupting people and degrading things." Get the picture?

I wonder if Paul had Psalm 101:3 in mind as he wrote to the Philippian believers. He challenged them to think about those things that were true (honest, upright, sincere, earnest), noble (dignified, majestic, awe-inspiring), right (just, reputable, righteous), pure (unadulterated by evil, free from defilement), lovely (pleasing), admirable (appealing or well-done), excellent (virtuous, outstanding in moral character), and praiseworthy. That's a tall order for us who live in a culture steeped with everything opposite of these traits. Nevertheless, that's our challenge.

You and I are surrounded by a sex-saturated society. In TV shows and newspaper ads, magazine articles and movie plots, impurity is rampant. No one is immune to the influences of these images, icons, and information. And if you continue to allow yourself to be immersed in what the world is telling you about sexuality, you will be affected—guaranteed. Why? Because you will begin to believe that what you're seeing on television and at the movies is real. Life on Wisteria Lane becomes the norm. A New York apartment occupied by a heterosexual woman and homosexual man becomes commonplace. The fallacies flaunted in the magazines and romance novels (even Christian romance!) will begin to permeate your thinking. Before long, you will begin to expect your husband to live up to your idealized expectation built up in your mind by what you've read. If he doesn't sweep you off of your feet in a romantic interlude after a hard day's work, then the romance must be gone from the marriage, and you must not be in love anymore. You could have a better life with the guy you know at work because he treats you better than your family does.

Can you see how easily sexual impurity can slip into your everyday life? Can you see how it can grow like a cancer when you don't run away from it? Scripture is clear—we are to stay away from immorality. Sadly, most of us flirt on the edge of disaster because we've become complacent to sexual impurity in its various forms.

How do you know if sexual impurity and immorality is creeping its way into your life? Take the following quiz to find out. Answer true or false:

_____ 1. When I browse through a magazine at the news stand, I thumb to articles focusing on "steamy bedroom secrets" or "ways to entice your man." Often, I buy the magazine.

_____ 2. Pornography can be found in my house or on my computer. It might not be mine, but it's there.

_____ 3. I have a favorite soap opera that I watch faithfully. (Yes, primetime soap operas count!)

_____ 4. I find myself wishing my husband would treat me like the guy in the chick flick treats his significant other.

_____ 5. I like to read romance novels and imagine myself as one of the chracters. (Yes, even Christian romance counts!)

_____ 6. I dress provocatively in public to get the attention of men.

_____ 7. I flirt with the guys at work (or church or soccer practice).

_____ 8. I have thought about leaving my husband because I don't feel like we're "in love" any more.

_____ 9. I continue to watch my favorite TV shows even though their content is questionable and immoral.

_____10. When convicted about my TV or movie habits, I make excuses like, "It's not really that bad," "You can't find a show without promiscuity," or "I tune out the bad stuff."

_____11. I hardly notice when sexual promiscuity is the theme of a book, magazine article, TV show, or movie. Even when I do notice, it doesn't bother me.

_____12. As a single mom, I've compromised my purity with a man I'm dating (or have dated).

_____13. I would be embarrassed if my pastor knew about the things I read, watch on TV, or see at the movies.

_____14. I fantasize about being with with another man (or woman).

_____15. It was difficult to be honest when taking this quiz.

Was it difficult to be honest? Was it painful to answer the last question truthfully? While some of these activities may seem harmless in isolation, they combine to form a lifestyle that accepts sexual impurity as the norm. If this quiz revealed more than you expected, don't get discouraged. Being honest about your present condition is the first step to real change.

If you want your daughter to live in purity, then you must model purity for her. She knows the TV shows you watch and is aware of the content; she sees the magazines you buy and the articles highlighted on the cover. She sees the way you dress, the way you flirt with the server at the restaurant, and the way you treat your husband. If you want to model purity, turn off the soap opera, read something more fruitful than a romance novel, quit dressing provocatively. If she doesn't see you flee from negative sexual images or behavior, why should she?

Can you still watch TV and maintain sexual purity? Yes. Can you still read books, go to the movies, and read articles online? Yes. It's tough, but it can be done. You must decide where you will draw a line in the sand. You must determine before God what you are willing to allow into your life and subsequently your heart and your actions.

Perhaps the greatest hope is that teenagers who "feel highly connected to their parents and report that their parents are warm, caring, and supportive" are far more likely to delay sexual activity than their peers."[10]

Our Greatest Hope

When it comes to sexual purity, our daughters will be faced with many challenges. In a society that often appears to be obsessed with sex, a teen's pursuit of maintaining sexual purity can be a rigorous swim upstream. Mothers must educate their daughters that God's call for sexual purity is not exclusive to sexual intercourse but to all sexual activity. Mothers should encourage their daughters to make a personal pledge to God to save sex for marriage, whether they do so through a formal program or privately before God. Mothers will need to remind their daughters on an ongoing basis of these truths through planned times of discussion and unplanned teachable moments.

Perhaps the greatest hope is that teenagers who "feel highly connected to their parents and report that their parents are warm, caring, and supportive" are far more likely to delay sexual activity than their peers."[10] Additionally, teenagers in grades 8 through 11 who perceive that their mothers disapprove of their engaging in sexual intercourse are more likely than their peers to delay sexual activity.[11] Clearly, mothers have great power in influencing their daughters to abstain from sex until marriage. We must articulate to our daughters that sexual activity outside of marriage is wrong and can have devastating physical, emotional, and spiritual consequences. We must also be quick to tell them that God created sex as something beautiful to be enjoyed in the confines of marriage. We must also model purity in every aspect of our own lives so that we can challenge our daughters to do the same.

1. http://www.cdc.gov/mmwr/preview/mmwrhtml/mm5138a2.htm.
2. http://www.usatoday.com/news/health/2003-06-03-teen-usat_x.htm.
3. National Campaign to Prevent Teen Pregnancy.
4. Seventeen, January 2003, 114.
5. Ibid.
6. Ibid.
7. Austin American Statesman, no date given.
8. Seventeen, January 2003, 115.
9. "Facts & Stats-1," National Campaign to Prevent Teen Pregnancy, 2002.
10. Henshaw, "U.S. Teenage Pregnancy Statistics."
11. Ibid.

TALKING POINTS

1. The next time you watch your favorite TV show with your daughter, talk about the sexual innuendos you see. Discuss whether the portrayal of sexuality is accurate or biblical.

2. As a family, talk about ways you've allowed impurity to invade your home. Think about jokes you tell, stores you frequent, movies you rent, and so forth. Determine alternative activities you can do that might be more in line with Philippians 4:8 or Psalm 101:3.

3. Talk to your daughter about rules for being online as they relate to sexual purity. Together, come up with a list of guidelines that she will follow while on the Internet.

4. Ask your daughter about the attitudes concerning sexual purity at her school. Gently prod her to open up by asking what students think about the hooking-up trend, oral sex, and the reputation of girls who are involved.

5. If appropriate, share with your daughter ways you may have compromised your sexual purity as a teenager. Spare her the details, though, and focus on what you wish you had done differently.

{76} *The Role of Fathers in Sexual Purity*

While a mother plays a huge role in guiding her daughter regarding sexual purity, you as her husband are also a role model. You need to communicate to your daughter as well. You may not deal with physiological things that are happening in the female body (many daughters would be mortified if their fathers took the lead in this discussion), but you can be proactive in helping her make the right choices about sex. Listed below are some principles and suggestions for you. Read them and then discuss them with your daughter.

1. RECOGNIZE YOUR ROLE.

It is important for you to be open with your daughter about sexuality. You are her protector and her spiritual leader. She sees you as a protector and her leader, and God has ordained you to be that for her. If you don't talk with her, and she ends up making wrong, life-altering, perhaps even tragic choices, you bear some responsibility. You need to talk to her about what goes on in the mind and body of a 16-year-old boy because you were one! You provide a unique perspective that your wife cannot offer. Further, there are some issues that, despite gender, you may be more comfortable in discussing. It is the dual responsibility for parents to discuss sexual purity; but because of personality style, upbringing, and other factors, you may be more comfortable discussing sexual purity.

2. MODEL SEXUAL PURITY IN YOUR OWN LIFE.

Your actions communicate volumes to your daughter. The way you treat other women will speak volumes. Your eyes communicate as well as your words. She watches what you do with your eyes when women pass by. She also listens to your comments to other men. She notices the kinds of movies you watch, especially those that have filthy language and portray sexual situations.

3. SHOW RESPECT FOR YOUR WIFE.

Remain faithfully committed to her alone. Your presence in the home can give your daughter a secure identity as a woman, especially if you applaud and support the feminine values you see in your wife and daughter(s).

4. PLAN A SPECIAL CEREMONY FOR YOUR DAUGHTER.

Partner with your wife to plan a special way to mark your daughter's transition into womanhood Perhaps, a party for her 13th or 16th birthday or a high school or college graduation celebration. Ideas for how men can be involved in their daughter's lives to address sexual purity and other matters are offered in *The Quest for Authentic Manhood,* session 23, "Fathers and Daughters" and in *Winning at Work and Home,* session 9, "Dad's Game Plan for Raising Sons and Daughters." Both of these resources are a part of the Men's Fraternity series. Go online to www.lifeway.com for more information.

5. TAKE A STAND ON MODESTY.

If it's too low, too short, or showing skin in the wrong places, say something about it and make her change before she leaves the house. But more importantly, explain to her why, which has to do with pleasing God and the way her clothing impacts others.

6. KEEP THE LINES OF COMMUNICATION OPEN.

Discussions about sexual purity are an ongoing dialogue, not a one-time event. Keep talking about the issue. What she deals with sexually at age 13 will be different from what she faces at age 17. Take advantage of teachable moments and don't rely on formal conversations you've arranged by appointment. Continue to develop a relationship with your daughter that involves trust. You cannot expect your daughter to talk with you about such an intimate and serious topic if you haven't built up a solid and trusting relationship.

A Mother's Journal

A Mother's Journal

The Cover Up

CAN THERE BE PURITY WITHOUT MODESTY?[1] This question was asked in the September 2001 issue of *Brio* magazine, which is published by Focus on the Family. The answer, of course, is no. Modesty and sexual purity go hand in hand. Given the current prevalence of immodest attire among girls, I felt the subject of modesty merits an entire chapter of this book.

Scantily Clad "Role Models"

The question submitted to the magazine regarding modesty and purity was asked specifically in reference to pop vocalist Jessica Simpson. She is an ex-pastor's daughter who went public with her commitment to remain a virgin until marriage. She has since married (and divorced), but her message of sexual purity was overshadowed by her immodest, anything-but-wholesome attire. Her decision to include a rendition of "His Eye Is on the Sparrow" on one of her CDs seems to conflict with her attire and, often, her behavior.

> *Our daughters have been bombarded with the "girl power" mantra that associates power and strength with a no-rules attitude in regard to clothes and behavior. The cultural powers-that-be know that "sex sells," and their bottom line is making the sale.*

Amazingly, she defended her immodest behavior and fashion choices in an interview in *Complete Woman* magazine. She was quoted as saying, "My soul and my faith are what's sexy about me."[2] I wasn't aware the one's "faith" could be sexy. Call it a hunch, but I'm not sure that's what God had in mind. Shouldn't our faith in God point to God rather than call attention to ourselves?

{ 82 }

Another scantily clad pop sensation who has had caused much heartache for mothers when shopping with their daughters is Britney Spears. Nora Schoenberg of the *Chicago Tribune* described Britney as the one "who made the bare midriff safe for the suburban preteen."[3] I remember how shocked I was when this trend kicked in and now, it hardly registers anymore. And if the shock has worn off for those of us who are mothers, the girls especially have become desensitized. When they couple a short tight shirt with low-rise jeans, it can make for a dangerous combination, especially when it comes to sitting down. Whereas, you and I have a natural tendency to pull our shirts down over our waistline when sitting, our girls do not. They seem to have no shame in flashing not only their midriffs, but also their thong underwear straps, and sometimes, even their backside. And we thought this look was exclusive to plumbers and TV repairmen!

The Fashion Message: Be Sexy

Fashion magazines, movies, and sitcoms have peddled the "be sexy" message to young women for quite some time. Unfortunately, the primary media influencers have now stooped to an all-time low by targeting elementary-aged girls. This negative influence has translated into clothes for little girls that reinforce the message to "be sexy" before most of them even know what the word means. "Being sexy" is equated with female empowerment or "girl power." Our daughters have been bombarded with the "girl power" mantra that associates power and strength with a no-rules attitude in regard to clothes and behavior. The cultural powers-that-be know that "sex sells," and their bottom line is making the sale.

Just recently, I was thumbing through the sale rack in the girl's department of a large department store. Another mother, within earshot, asked the sales clerk for assistance in choosing an outfit for her 10-year-old daughter for an upcoming party. The sales clerk plucked an item off my rack and proceeded to hold up a sheer blouse for the mother's approval. The mother said, "That blouse is see-through." The sales clerk responded, "Have her wear a sports bra underneath. This is what all the girls her age are wearing." By now I am practically hyperventilating, as I often do when I feel an onslaught of uninvited words threatening to spew out of my mouth. The floodgates burst, and I belted out: "She's going to a *party*, for heaven's sakes, not a strip club—she's 10 years old!" The sales clerk stormed off, and the mother proceeded to thank me for confirming what she already knew.

Unfortunately, not all mothers agree. Someone has to be buying this stuff or the stores wouldn't be overrun with clothes fit for diva-wannabes. Many mothers have discounted the clothing battle as a battle not worth fighting. Others fear their daughters might not be popular if they don't don the latest skin-baring fashions. I have to prepare myself every afternoon before pulling into the parking lot to pick up my son from school. It's all I can do to refrain from screaming, "Cover up, chica!" to some of the girls walking past my car. I'm told that the school has a dress code, but apparently no one is enforcing it.

The school parking lot is not the only place where I've had to hold my tongue. The midriff-baring fashions have even made their way into many of our churches. We need to extend grace to young ladies visiting our churches who may be unaware of appropriate apparel guidelines, but Christian girls and their parents should know better! In an article in *The New York Times* called "Dressing Down for Summer Worship," one Catholic church has had to resort to dress-up guidelines for parishioners volunteering as liturgical ministers. The guidelines were developed, the article said, "after a teenage girl walked down the center aisle in a procession at Sunday Mass, holding high the book of the Gospel while wearing short shorts and a midriff-baring halter."[4]

At a large Christian youth event where I was a designated parent chaperone, I was appalled to see girls as young as middle school parading around in jeans so tight you could see the date of a dime in their back pockets. Others had bare midriffs or plunging necklines. Clearly many Christian girls have become desensitized by the saturation of sexually provocative fashions and, thus, have conformed to the world. While I am disappointed to find that many Christian girls have rationalized wearing inappropriate apparel to the Lord's house (or anywhere else for that matter), I find it especially disturbing that most have Christian parents who, for whatever reasons, apparently have turned their heads and allowed their daughters to dress immodestly.

In your opinion, can there be purity without modesty? Why or why not?

What are some examples of clothing you have seen recently that send the message "Be sexy"?

Who are some cultural icons your daughter looks up to? How do these pop sensations dress? How have you seen your daughter imitate these role models in the way she dresses?

Have you witnessed examples of immodest clothing in your church? If so, why do you think parents allow their daughters to dress inappropriately in church?

How can we in the church communicate to non-Christian girls the need for appropriate attire?

God's Perspective on Modesty

Our daughters should be taught early on not to conform to the pattern of this world but instead to be transformed to God's pattern by renewing their minds. In doing so, they will be able to test and approve what God's good, pleasing, and perfect will is (see Rom. 12:2). When discovering God's will—even regarding modesty—the best place to look is God's Word, the Bible.

Read Ephesians 5:8-9.

According to this passage, what were we before we became believers?
What are we now?

What is the command in this passage?

What does it mean to "walk as children of light"?

What is the fruit of living in the light? How might these be manifested in the way we dress?

In the space below, compare the fruit of walking in the light versus walking in darkness (see Eph. 5:3-5).

In Ephesians 5:8, Christians are challenged to "walk as children of light." We've been rescued from the darkness. As believers, our lives should reflect the fact that we no longer belong to the darkness. Our behavior should be different from those still trapped in the darkness. We're not supposed to live just like everyone else. The issue of nonconformity is so important. We are supposed to act; believe; think; and, yes, dress differently from those who do not know Christ. Does this mean that we should dress in colorless smocks from head to toe? No, although it would make shopping and getting ready for school a whole lot easier! Being a follower of Christ does mean, however, that even our dress should bring honor to God instead of attention to ourselves.

Read 1 Timothy 2:9-10. While this passage discusses proper apparel for worship, it provides good guidelines for modesty in general.

According to this passage, how did Paul instruct women to dress for worship?

What were the women to avoid wearing?

What were they instead to adorn themselves with?

How can you adorn yourself with good works? What might that look like in a believer's life?

What is the result of living in such a manner?

Paul wrote the Letter to Timothy, his young protégé and son in the faith. Timothy had remained in Ephesus to deal with certain problems in the church. Because Christianity was birthed in a pagan world, the church struggled at times with its identity and character. The church Timothy pastored needed to develop a sense of order, peace, and holiness. Paul wanted the church's behavior to reflect the character of God; its members should reflect God's character in their behavior.

First Timothy 2:9-10 cautions against elaborate hairstyles, gold, pearls, or expensive clothes. Commentaries indicate that women of the East spent much time styling their hair and, according to the prevailing fashion of the time, plaited it with great care, arranging it in various styles and often ornamenting it with silver wires or spangles. Apparently, these particular styles were disrupting and interfering with worship. Perhaps some women in Ephesus were flaunting their dress and jewelry in front of poor women.

The verses are not to be taken literally in the sense of forbidding the wearing of braided hair, jewelry, or nice clothes in today's world. Rather, they stand as a warning not to emulate the women of the world whose attention tends to be devoted to appearance rather than godly deeds. Once again Christians are called to be set apart from the world. The overarching principle is one of focus: does a person glorify God or self? In other words, your (or your teen's) outward appearance should not conflict with inner character.

The Greek word for "modest" is *kosmios*. It relates to ornamentation or decoration, and it means that which is "well ordered." One commentary says, "The true idea here is, that her attention to her appearance should be such that she will be offensive to no class of persons; such as to show that her mind is supremely fixed on higher and more important things."[5] The Greek word for "propriety" is *sophrosune*, which means "sanity" or "soundness of mind." Let me translate that for you in the context of our discussion: Do the clothes I purchase for my daughter indicate soundness of mind or that I've lost my mind?

Women professing to worship God should focus more on adorning themselves with godly deeds. Barnes' Commentary says this: "It is not appropriate for women who profess to be the followers of the Saviour, to seek to be distinguished for personal, external decorations. If they are Christians, they have seen the vanity of these things, and have fixed the heart on more substantial realities. They are professed followers of Him 'who went about doing good,' and the performance of good works especially becomes them. They profess to have fixed the affections on God their Saviour, and to be living for heaven; and it is not becoming in them to seek such ornaments as would indicate that the heart is supremely attached to worldly things."[6]

When Paul wrote the verses pertaining to the proper apparel of women in worship, his main concern was that nothing would serve to distract from God during a worship service. Everything about a church service should point to God—the music, the sermon, everything. This is not just a caution against immodest clothing but rather against any outfit that would distract attention from God.

Think about the clothes you have purchased for your daughter or have allowed her to wear. Do any of these clothes bring dishonor to God?

Do your daughter's clothes conflict with her inner character? Do her clothes reflect a pure heart? Why or why not? What does your daughter draw attention to—herself or God?

Guys and Modesty

When discussing modesty and the attention girls attract with their dress, we must address the importance of dressing modestly for the opposite sex. We all know that when it comes to sexuality, girls and guys are wired differently. Guys are more visually stimulated, while girls are more emotionally stimulated. Case in point: It would make my day to hear my husband say, "Honey, I want to get into your world. Let's go to dinner and talk, and then let's go shopping and get you something." It would make my husband's day (or night) just to see me wear something other than his oversized T-shirts to bed. I think you get my point.

In an Austin, Texas, newspaper article addressing immodest fashions, a sampling of boys at a local mall were interviewed and asked what they thought of the girls who walked by wearing the latest skin-baring fashions. One boy suggested that girls "show more to get attention." Another boy perceived it as an "invitation." He said, "They're telling you, 'Come get it.' When girls dress like that, it tells guys they're easy."[7] What mom and dad, given that news flash, would allow their daughter to leave the house in an outfit that screams, "Come and get it!" to every red-blooded male that crosses her path? Sorry, but my daughter is not going to be branded an "invitation" in the name of fashion.

In my book for teen girls *TeenVirtue: Real Issues, Real Life: A Teen Girl's Survival Guide,* we polled Christian guys across the nation and asked this question, "If you could give girls one piece of honest advice, what would it be?" Here are some of my favorite responses regarding dress:

"I would tell girls that if they knew how guys' and men's minds work, they would be more careful about what they wear—like halter tops and shirts showing your belly." (Corey, 18)

"Some girls need to put more clothes on." (Jacob, 14)

"I personally would tell girls to be more modest, stop the cursing, and remember their morals." (Caleb, 15)

And my personal favorite: *"If I could give girls one piece of advice, it would be simply to dress modestly and please do not wear tight shirts that show your stomach. Seriously, who wants to see that? Just wear clothes that allow a guy to keep his mind and attention focused on the amazing girl you are on the inside."* (Kyle, 17)

I am certainly not excusing inappropriate behavior among young men. As parents, we should be equally diligent in raising our sons to respect young women and place a higher value on what they see on the inside rather than what they see on the outside. However, we cannot change the fact that guys are visually stimulated and inclined to read more into a racy outfit than a simple expression of fashion. As a parent, you must help your daughter understand the impact of her outfits on the hormones of a teenage boy (or adult male).

Living by Example

It is important to help our daughters understand that their clothing should honor God and reflect His character; we should also help our daughters grasp how guys' interpret their dress. However, as a mother, it is vitally important for you to recognize the role you play in your daughter's choice of clothing. If you as a mother are not setting the example by dressing modestly, then you cannot expect your daughter (or her friends) to follow suit.

Remember this: your actions carry consequences to others. In Romans 14:21, Paul challenged believers not to do anything that would cause another person to stumble spiritually. In the context of our situation, think of it this way: like mother, like daughter. If you wear short skirts, she will wear micro-minis, too. If you bare your midriff, go without a bra, or don the latest cleavage-baring fashion, so will she. Think about the quotes from guys on the previous page. How do you want your daughter to be perceived? How do you want men to look at her? What thoughts do you want men and boys to think about your daughter? If you want your daughter to be honored and respected, then provide for her an example of dressing with modesty and good sense. Your priority is not to be considered the cool or hip mother or to bid for the attraction and attention of men. Your priority is to guide your daughter to dress in a way that pleases God.

> *Your priority is not to be considered the cool or hip mother or to bid for the attraction and attention of men. Your priority is to guide your daughter to dress in a way that pleases God.*

I am certainly not saying that those of us in our 30's, 40's, and beyond should be sentenced to a closet full of holiday-themed sweaters and Naturalizer footwear. I myself am not a Talbots-kind-of-gal. I recently purchased a pair of jeans from Banana Republic, and the first time I wore them, at least 10 friends asked me if I had lost weight. Apparently, the low-rise style is more flattering to my shape, which of course, makes Banana Republic my new favorite store. But, I am not naïve enough to couple the jeans with a cute midriff-baring tee. I do my once-a-month crunches just like the rest of my post-40-year-old soccer-mom friends. The exercise is usually brought on suddenly while watching an episode of *Extreme Makeover* and abandoned just as suddenly when the Cool Ranch Doritos® ad runs midway through the show. I'm not ashamed of my body, and I'm not trying to communicate that you should be ashamed of the way God created you. But the bottom line is this: bare midriffs belong in the privacy of your bedroom, not in public. There is nothing wrong with donning the latest fashions, but do so in good taste.

Think about your clothing styles and choices. How have you dressed according to the standards of the world instead of God's Word? What clothes need to come out of the closet to go into the trash? Before you read another word, go to your closet right now. Demonstrate your commitment to your daughter's modesty and purity and get rid of clothes that do not set a positive example for your daughter to follow.

Teaching Self-Respect

When you teach your daughter to dress modestly, you're teaching her to respect herself—a lost art in today's culture. Many girls dress immodestly to gain attention from guys, while others innocently have bought into the current immodest fashion trend without seeing the harm. Teen girls struggle with their sense of self-worth and value. To solve that struggle, culture screams that their sense of self-worth can be boosted by dressing to lure. By modeling modesty and setting standards for your daughter to follow, you are teaching her that she should be treated with honor and respect. Her body is not for display or to be the object of a guys' impure thoughts. She is worth much more than that. Her value stems from something much deeper than the latest line of immodest fashion. Just like a label on a product, our girls need to know that their clothes make a statement—a statement, perhaps, that is not a true reflection of their hearts, one they never intended to send.

Setting the Standards

If you have never had a discussion with your daughter about appropriate clothes, you'll need to set some guidelines. (Keep in mind that if you've never set boundaries before, your daughter is likely to rebel against the new standards of decency!) Before the next shopping trip, set firm standards with your daughter regarding appropriate and inappropriate clothing. Come up with some helpful guidelines to follow when selecting clothes. For example, T-shirts cover your waistband, no cleavage showing, no exposed bra straps, no micro-minis, and no jeans tight enough to see the date of a dime in your back pocket. And I know I speak on behalf of those of us with sons—wear a bra!

Here are some questions you and your daughter can ask when shopping or looking in front of the mirror. If the answer to these questions is yes, then an outfit change or adaptation is in order. Always explain the why behind the guidelines you have set. That goes beyond the standard, "Because I said so!" Setting clear standards before you go shopping (or your daughter goes to the mall) will prevent you from becoming "fashion police" when your daughter is leaving the house. Not to mention, it may eliminate some embarrassing knock-down-drag-outs in the store if you shop together.

SHIRTS
- When I wear a loose or scoop-neck shirt, can I see anything when I lean over?
- Does my stomach show when I raise my hands above my head?
- Is my shirt too tight?
- Is this top so sheer that others can see my bra?
- When I wear a sleeveless shirt, do the arm holes gape and show my bra?
- Does this shirt have sexually suggestive slogans?

PANTS
- Do I have to suck in my stomach to zip my paints?
- Do these jeans ride so low that my panties show?
- Are these jeans or pants too tight? Do they show every curve? Do they show every outline of my panties?

SKIRTS AND SHORTS
- Do the slits on this skirt (if applicable) come too far up my leg? Do they show too much when I walk?
- Do these shorts reveal my panty line?
- Is my skirt see-through? If so, it needs a slip.

Above all else, remind your daughter that her clothing choices are a reflection of her heart and intentions. Encourage her to get in the habit of doing a dressing room mirror check and asking herself, "Would I be comfortable standing before God in this outfit?"

What's a Mother to Do?

Now that we're all fighting mad, what can mothers do to counteract the current immodest fashion trend? For starters, we can speak up. You may {93} remember a JCPenney commercial advertising their line of denim hipster jeans. In the commercial a girl yanks on her jeans, and her mother is aghast. "You can't go to school looking like that," the mother says sternly. The mother then pulls the pants down lower. After numerous complaints, JCPenney announced they were pulling the commercial with the following statement: "JCPenney respects the values that parents instill in their children as they develop and, in making this decision, underscored that it considers important the opinions of its customers nationwide."[8] In a similar incident, Abercrombie & Fitch pulled their line of thong underwear for young girls after a barrage of complaints from parents. Never think your voice doesn't matter.

I have scrapped with the clothing industry on several occasions. Recently, I e-mailed Mervyns department stores regarding a sales flier that I received in the mail. It highlighted a brand called "Teaze" for young girls. I have boycotted Abercrombie & Fitch for years and will continue to do so until they cease selling items that commonly portray women as objects. Tim Wildmon, president of the American Family Association, makes the point that "Abercrombie & Fitch does not merely sell a popular line of clothing—they sell a lifestyle."[9]

I make it a point to share my disappointment in the lack of modest clothing with store managers, as well as pay my compliments to managers that carry modest clothing. Sometimes I wonder if my voice will make a difference, but I will persevere for the sake of my daughter—and yours.

Stores are overrun with clothes fit more for future strippers than little girls. A simple mother-daughter shopping expedition can be discouraging. We may have to look harder and shop longer, but it is possible to find clothes for our daughters that are both stylish and modest. Our daughters do not need to look like nuns every time they head outdoors, but they do need to dress in such a way that brings honor and glory to God. I have drawn a firm boundary when it comes to what my daughter is and is not allowed to wear. Paige is allowed to wear most styles of jeans as long as they are not tight and her shirt overlaps her waistline. If the waist in the pants is big, she wears a belt. She cannot wear short shorts or spaghetti strap shirts with exposed bra straps. Clothing conflicts are few because I have carefully supported my modesty standard with the reasons given in this chapter. Dressing with decency and propriety may not earn her a fashion award, but in the end, purity of the heart is the most prized adornment.

What's a Daughter to Do?

In addition, teach your daughter to speak out. Girls that band together and speak with a unified voice cannot be ignored. Just recently, a group of girls from Pennsylvania organized a "girlcott" of Abercrombie & Fitch because of a line of T-shirts that the clothing maker sold. Some of the offending shirts read: "Who needs brains when you have these?" "Anatomy Tutor," "I'd look great on you," and "Blondes Are Adored, Brunettes Are Ignored." Their story caught the attention of CBS and CNN, which both told the girls' story. The girls (and all the negative publicity) were able to persuade Abercrombie & Fitch to remove the offensive shirts from their shelves.[10] Clearly, clothing manufacturers need not only the financial support, but also the public endorsement of their products. Challenge your daughters and her friends to speak out. Their voices matter!

1. Brio, September 2001.
2. Complete Woman, October-November 2002, 7.
3. Nora Schoenberg, "Take It Off, Britney," Chicago Tribune, 26 August 2002, 1.
4. Francine Parnes, "Dressing Down for Summer Worship," The New York Times, 24 August 2002.
5. Barnes' Commentary, electronic database. Biblesoft, 1997.
6. Ibid.
7. Ricardo Gandara, "What girls wear, and what boys think," Austin American Statesman, 22 April 2001.
8. Emily Wax, "Parents Can't Bear Girl's Skimpy Attire," Washingtonpost.com, 11 August 2001.
9. American Family Association Journal, September 2003.
10. "Bawdy T-shirts set off "girlcott" by teens," 3 November 2005, post-gazette.com Lifestyle, http://www.post-gazette.com/pg/05307/599884.stm.

TALKING POINTS

1. Look for teachable moments to discuss modesty with your daughter. These might include seeing an inappropriate outfit at the mall, on a television show, or while traveling in the car together.

2. Discuss together the guidelines you will set for clothing you will and will not allow your daughter to wear. Be specific and include issues such as bare midriffs, see-through clothing, length of shorts and miniskirts. Use the questions listed in this chapter to help you create guidelines. Include your husband in this discussion because his involvement will speak volumes to your daughter.

3. Discuss with your daughter the answer to this question: What statement do my clothes make about my heart? Make sure that both of you answer this question honestly. Based on your answer, commit to make changes in your wardrobe selection.

4. Talk with your daughter about the guys' comments on page 89. Ask her what the guys around her would say about the way she dresses.

A Mother's Journal

A Mother's Journal

CHAPTER 6

Prince Charming: Fact or Fairy Tale?

THE CINDERELLA STORY is played out over and over again in romance novels, on television, and on the silver screen. Often the top-grossing movies are nothing more than modern-day versions of the Cinderella story. These movies are dubbed "chick flicks" because they are marketed directly to girls and women who have a soft spot for romance. Producers know that grown-up adaptations of the Cinderella story translate into big bucks. Women rationalize that seven dollars is a small price to pay to retreat into fairy-tale land and observe the world as they believe it should be.

Woe to the poor male who is subjected to the latest chick flick. My son recently attended the latest Cinderella story with a group of friends. He came home dazed and confused and offered the following movie review: "All the girls loved it, and I can't figure out why. The entire movie builds up to this couple getting together. By the end of the movie, they finally get together, and all the girls in our group acted so surprised. It was the dumbest movie I've ever seen." Bless his heart. He has so much to learn.

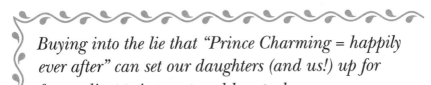

Buying into the lie that "Prince Charming = happily ever after" can set our daughters (and us!) up for future disappointment and heartache.

Each chick flick comes complete with a standard Cinderella, who is perfectly adorable yet noticeably lacking something or, more appropriately, someone. Enter Prince Charming (played by the latest Hollywood hunk), who at some point during the movie realizes that Cinderella is, in fact, perfectly adorable and that he alone holds the key to providing her with perfect love and happiness. The remainder of the story centers on his pursuit to capture her heart. Living "happily ever after" is only a kiss away. Mission accomplished. The end. The credits on the screen roll, and in our minds, time stands still with the kiss and the perfect life that we are led to believe will follow.

The Desire for Happily Ever After

While there is nothing inherently wrong with our daughters dreaming about the day their Prince Charming will come, we, as mothers, must help them separate fantasy from reality. Buying into the lie that "Prince Charming = happily ever after" can set our daughters (and us!) up for future disappointment and heartache.

Read Proverbs 19:22a in several different translations. (You can look online for different translations if you don't have any on hand.) Then in the space below, paraphrase this verse in your own words.

Do you think this desire is universal for every person? Why or why not?

How would you know if you had encountered this type of love?

Have you ever encountered this? Describe your experience .

One translation renders this verse as, "A man's desire should be loyalty to the covenant" (HCSB), while others say, "What a man desires is unfailing love" (NIV). Others say, "What is desired in a man is kindness" (NKJV), "What matters most is loyalty" (CEV), and "Loyalty makes a person attractive" (NLT). There's something within our hearts that craves a love that will be faithful. We long to encounter a love that won't betray us, let us down, or leave us longing for more. While this longing may be more disguised among men, it is laid bare in the hearts of women. We long to be loved, wooed, nurtured, and held safe by a love that will not let us go. Much of the appeal that keeps women flocking to the fairy tale-themed movies and buying romance novels is the thought that one perfect man exists who will love them unconditionally without fail. Media types from Hollywood to Harlequin have figured out how to market to a woman's desire for "unfailing love."

While I don't endorse the movie *Jerry McGuire,* it illustrates a major fallacy in today's culture. The main character (played by Tom Cruise) is in an elevator with Dorothy, a love interest (played by Rene Zelweger). A hearing-impaired couple get on the elevator with Jerry and Dorothy, and they begin signing to each other. It becomes obvious that they are in love. Before they leave the elevator, the man signs in a way that catches Jerry's attention. Offhandedly, he says, "I wonder what he just said." Dorothy replies, "My favorite aunt is hearing impaired. He just said 'You complete me.'" Later on, in a climactic moment at the end of the movie, Jerry proclaims, "You complete me," as a pledge of his love and need for Dorothy, the woman he has fallen for. And true to the formula, this couple lives happily ever after because they've found the one who makes them complete.

The quote "you complete me" is disturbing because it is a blatant lie. No one person can ever make another person complete. Women have been convinced that the hole in their hearts can be filled by a person. We've bought into the lie that there's a "special someone" out there who can meet all our needs, fulfill every fantasy, and make us whole and complete. It's a lie we've been fed since we heard the story of Cinderella for the first time. And unfortunately, our daughters are hearing this message loud and clear. As a result, they are searching for that perfect someone, going from boyfriend to boyfriend in the quest to find Mr. Right. They often jump from relationship to relationship in a serial dating scenario that leaves nothing but heartache, emptiness, and insecurity in the wake. Unless they learn the source of love, they will never be satisfied. They are searching for something that cannot be found in a human being. It can only be found in God.

On a recent morning, I stood in line at my favorite coffee shop. On a chalkboard behind the checkout was written the following question as a brain teaser: "What is the meaning of life?" When it was my turn to order, I politely asked the cashier, who looked to be around college age, "Are you planning to post the answer tomorrow?" She grinned and said, "Well, I suppose the answer is different for everyone." I turned the question back on her and asked her what she considered to be the meaning of life. She quickly said, "The meaning of life is love." I challenged her with the answer, "That's a shame, since the divorce rate is over 50 percent and those who marry usually do so for love." Obviously, our culture doesn't understand that life's meaning does not begin or end in the love of another person.

The Filler of Our Hearts

Before our girls feel that first pitter-patter in their hearts that might be misinterpreted as "true love," we must help them define true love. We must educate them to the fact that no man can love them perfectly except One. We must tell them that God purposely placed a desire within their hearts to be loved perfectly and completely. In placing this desire on their hearts, the goal was that they would be drawn to Him as the only source that could satisfy their desire for unfailing love. Unfortunately, many girls and women (including Christians) miss this truth and hold out for Prince Charming.

Fortunately, Scripture proclaims loudly the depth and magnitude of God's love. Let's look at a few passages that tell us about a love that will not leave us longing.

Read Ephesians 1:4-5.

What words or phrases give clues about God's love for you?

What does it mean to be "holy"? To be "blameless"?

According to this passage, why did He adopt us?

These two small verses provide great insight into God's love for us. The Message paraphrases these verses to say, "Long before he laid down earth's foundations, he had us in mind, had settled on us as the focus of his love, to be made whole and holy by his love. Long, long ago he decided to adopt us into his family through Jesus Christ." Take a few minutes and ponder the wonder of these verses. The God of the universe, the One without beginning or end, decided long before He even created the world to make you and me the object of his affection. In Him and in His love, we are made whole—complete, without fault, without blemish, without defect. And without Him, we can never be all we were created to be because we were designed and fashioned for a relationship with our Creator. The problem with humanity is that we spend all our energy, time, money, and heart on filling up the hole in our hearts that was designed to be filled by God alone.

Listed below are things that people pursue in an effort to fill the void in their hearts instead of turning to God. Check the ones you've foolishly pursued.

- [ ] career
- [ ] beauty
- [ ] approval of others
- [ ] shopping
- [ ] money
- [ ] power
- [ ] sexual pleasure
- [ ] children
- [ ] car
- [ ] status
- [ ] alcohol
- [ ] jewelry
- [ ] relationship
- [ ] good deeds
- [ ] television
- [ ] physical fitness

What happened when you pursued those things?

Which of these pursuits do you still struggle with at times?

In today's culture it's easy to get drawn away from God's love. We listen to the voices around us that tell us where to find love, joy, contentment, and peace. We begin to believe that God's love can't be the answer—it is too good to be true. We rationalize that no one could ever love us with such a pure love. And no person can. But God can. In fact, He proclaims His faithful love over and over again in Scripture, in both the Old Testament and the New Testament.

Read the following verses. Summarize what they say about God's love.

Deuteronomy 33:26-27 _____

_____

Psalm 13:5-6_____

_____

Psalm 130:7 _____

_____

Psalm 136_____

_____

Isaiah 54:10 _____

_____

Lamentations 3:22-23 _____

_____

Zephaniah 3:17 _____

_____

Romans 8:38-39_____

_____

1 John 3:16; 4:9-10_____

_____

1 John 4:18 _____

_____

Revelation 1:5b-6 _____

_____

From the earliest moments in Scripture, we see God's love in action. In love He provided covers for Adam and Eve even after they had sinned against Him (Gen. 3:21). Deuteronomy records a hymn of praise to the God who would fight for the Israelites and guard over them (Deut. 32). The Psalms are filled with declarations of His love—a love that is good, that provides full redemption, and that endures forever. The prophets spoke of His love that would remain steadfast, even "though the mountains move and the hills shake, My love will not be removed from you and My covenant of peace will not be shaken" (Isa. 54:10). Even in times of lament, people could still rely on God's love that is new every morning. In this great love the Lover of our souls would quiet us with His love and rejoice over us with singing. How can we not respond in love to a God who would actually sing for joy over us?

The ultimate demonstration of God's relentless, untamable, remarkable love is in the sacrifice of His Son on our behalf. Jesus proclaimed the depth of His love. Paul further proclaimed its measure in the Book of Romans, proclaiming that nothing in all of creation—nothing in our past, our present, or even our future—could get between us and God's love.

Knowing the Unknowable

Pondering the scope of God's love is cause for praise and worship at the feet of the One who would choose us as the apple of His eye. A lifetime could not afford enough time for you and me to experience the depths of His love. Yet Paul prayed for such a thing.

Read Ephesians 3:17-19.

What was Paul's prayer for the Ephesian church?

Draw a symbol to illustrate God's love as Paul described it.

In verse 19, How did Paul characterize God's love?

According to verse 19, what results when we experience God's love?

Take a sneak peak at verses 20-21. How did Paul end this chapter?

Why do you think Paul broke out into praise?

Use the journal space at the end of this chapter to express your feelings about His love by writing your own hymn of praise.

Paul prayed that the Ephesian believers (and we) would know the length, width, height, and depth of God's love. He even prayed a peculiar thing: that we would know the Messiah's love, a love that surpasses knowledge. Did you catch that? In one breath Paul prayed that you and I might know the depths of God's love. And in the next breath He recognizes that we can never exhaust the limits of His love. Who would not want to know and experience a love that surpasses knowledge?

We are well on our way to knowing that amazing love when we acknowledge that only by Christ are we "filled to the measure of the fullness of God." The words *filled* and *fullness* are derived from the Greek word, *pleroo*, which means to "level up (a hollow)" or "complete." Only the love of Christ can fill and complete our hearts (and the hearts of our daughters). Failure to recognize this revolutionary truth leads many girls and women to assume falsely that completion is found in other things, especially relationships with the opposite sex. Young ladies who falsely assume that relationships can provide the completion their hearts long for are more likely to experience sexual promiscuity, unhealthy dating relationships, and, eventually, failed marriages than are those young ladies who understand that only God can fill and complete their hearts through a personal relationship with Jesus Christ.

Because I had failed to realize and accept that Jesus Christ was the only one who could level up the hollow places in my heart, I attempted over the years to fill the void in my heart with various worldly solutions, including dating relationships.

Learning the Lesson Early

Young women who recognize that only Jesus Christ has the power to level up the hollow places within their hearts are better equipped to exercise caution when it comes to matters of their hearts. As mothers we must take advantage of teachable moments to impart and reinforce this critical truth with our daughters. We must be purposeful in defining true love according to God's definition if our daughters are to reject the world's lie that "Prince Charming = happily ever after." Life is not a fairy tale, especially concerning matters of the heart.

Unfortunately, most mothers do not begin to address matters of the heart with their daughters until they are crying on their shoulders after a painful breakup. I was totally caught off guard when my oldest child, Ryan, entered the "going out with girls" phase. I vividly recall chaperoning a seventh-grade dance and glancing out on the dance floor only to see my son slow dancing with a girl and, of all things, enjoying it! I didn't know whether to laugh or to cry. (For the record, I went out to my car, called my husband on my cell phone, and cried!) It was clear that Ryan had more than noticed girls and had entered a new phase of life. I felt grossly unprepared to deal with the hormones that would follow. Part of me was excited to see him start to round the corner of adolescence, and the other part of me wanted to retreat to the days of reading his favorite Dr. Seuss book over and over again.

Now that my daughter has entered the same phase, I don't feel much more qualified, but I have made it my personal mission to remind her often of the love of God that surpasses all knowledge. The challenge seems especially overwhelming when I reflect back on my own tumultuous transition into adolescence. By default, I bought into the fairy-tale lie that eternal happiness was directly linked to finding my Prince Charming or one perfect soul mate. Because I had failed to realize and accept that Jesus Christ was the only one who could level up the hollow places in my heart, I attempted over the years to fill the void in my heart with various worldly solutions, including dating relationships. Many of my Christian friends seemed to be on the same search, somehow failing to grasp how wide and long and high and deep is the love of Christ. Like me, they also longed for filling and completion of their hearts and, instead, settled for the world's counterfeit. Our daughters will run the same risk unless we help them become rooted and established in God's love before they start seeking love through relationships with boys. Our daughters will have a healthier view of relationships with the opposite sex if the process of teaching them about God's love is set in place long before they bat an eyelash at their first crush.

My children have been blessed by growing up in a Christian home. They go to a wonderful Christian school, and are involved in a Bible-believing church. Sometimes I worry that they hear the message of God's unfailing love so often that they may take it for granted and look to the world's brand of love for satisfaction. I take advantage of teachable moments to point out how Christians can easily make the mistake of substituting the love of Christ with a worldly counterfeit brand of love, only to come up short in the end. While I want them to experience the joy of meeting that one special person, falling in love, and getting married (if God so wills), most importantly, I want them to find their completion in Christ. My prayer is that they come to a place where they are awestruck by His love. Only then will they be able to properly define true love.

Love and Marriage

While the futures of our daughters will probably include meeting and marrying their Prince Charming, we must tell them well in advance that this prince is not responsible for providing them with a life lived "happily ever after." It is unfair and unreasonable to place the large burden for their personal happiness on another person. Living happily ever after is {109} a personal choice. Healthy and happy marriages require time and hard work from both parties. They come as a result of a husband and wife loving each other with the love of Jesus Christ. Our culture and, at times, the Christian community often link marriage as the key to a life lived happily ever after.

Many women have learned this lesson the hard way. They may be believers and may even seek after God's heart, but they feel discontent in their marriages. They have bought into the lie that their husbands would complete them, satisfy them, and make them whole. Living in that lie, these women have created a set of expectations for their husbands that can never be satisfied. And because husbands are human and fallible, these women have become disappointed, disillusioned, and disheartened that their Prince Charming doesn't always meet their needs.

Think about your own marriage. Describe in the journal space at the end of this chapter a time when your husband didn't live up to your expectations (For example: "My husband didn't encourage me when I lost my job;" "My husband didn't compliment me when I lost weight;" or, "He doesn't make me feel good anymore"). Also describe how you felt when he didn't live up to your expectations.

If you'll look carefully behind that experience, you might find that your husband wasn't the main problem. His inadequacies really weren't the issue. The problem might have been in your expectation of him to meet every need of your heart. I'm not letting husbands off the hook; they should give us love. However, they are not responsible for making us feel complete and whole! The marriage relationship is a model of the depth of God's love, but it is not a replacement for it. While the healthiest marriages will bring great joy, they will not come close to the satisfaction that comes when we experience the unfailing love of Christ.

Unless our daughters have reconciled that God created the longing in their hearts to be loved and that He provided His Son as the primary means to quench that longing, they are setting themselves up for disappointment and disillusionment in relationships with the opposite sex in the future. It is unreasonable to expect that any mortal man can satisfy a divinely inspired longing of the heart with a man-made brand of love. Let us also be reminded that investing in a healthy marriage will benefit for a lifetime, while investing in a relationship with Christ will benefit for eternity. Jesus made clear in Mark 12:25 that there will be no marriages in heaven. Our daughters must be taught that investing in a close and personal relationship with Jesus Christ is a priority, not to mention a prerequisite to investing in a happy marriage.

The longer our daughters spend basking in the unfailing love of Christ, the better equipped they will be in the future to explore other matters of the heart. As mothers, we have a call to build a fence of protection around our daughters' hearts until the love of Christ has penetrated their hearts through and through. The good news: There is One Perfect Man who will complete them. His name is Jesus. Only when our daughters grasp how wide and long and high and deep is the love of Christ and are filled to the measure of the fullness of God will they discover the meaning of "happily ever after."

End this chapter by praying Ephesians 3:17-19 for your daughter: "And I pray that _____, being rooted and firmly established in love, may be able to comprehend with all the saints what is the length and width, height and depth of God's love, and to know the Messiah's love that surpassses knowledge so you may be filled with all the fullness of God."

TALKING POINTS

1. Discuss with your daughter the myth that a man or marriage leads to "happily ever after," and explain the purpose of marriage in the eyes of God. Stress that achieving "happily ever after" in marriage is an individual choice.

2. Write Ephesians 3:17-19 on a note card. Insert your daughter's name in the verse and commit to pray it on a regular basis. Print the verse out for your daughter and help her memorize it. Be sure to explain the meaning behind the verse.

3. Listen to the audio segment for this session contained on the CD in the back of this book. Then talk with your daughter about the types of dating she needs to avoid (dating for fun, dating by emotion, joined-at-the-hip dating, and "mission field" dating). If possible, tell your daughter about a time you were lured into dating for one of these wrong reasons. Also share the consequences you faced.

4. If your daughter is an older teenager, read together the book *Captivating* by John and Stasi Eldredge. Go out for coffee or hang out in a place your daughter enjoys and talk about how well the book captures the hearts of women.

Taking Your Daughter on Dates

As a father, you model for your daughter how a man should treat a woman. The way you treat your wife speaks to your daughter, and her choices in dating relationships probably will be patterned in part by the example you have set. She can also learn how a guy is supposed to treat a girl by the way you treat her. To help foster this relationship, commit to take your daughter on regular "dates." When you go out, open doors for her. Pay for the activity (if it involves money). Let her order food first. Pull out chairs so she can sit down. Listen attentively when she talks. Refrain from trying to "fix" problems she may have. Walk her to the front door. Offer her your jacket if she gets cold. Be a servant. In modeling a healthy dating situation, you are setting the standard for other men to follow. If you treat her with love, dignity, and respect, she will be more likely to date men who are willing to treat her as you did. Listed below are some ideas for dates with your daughter. Some require little money or time. Others require both. She needs to learn that spending time together doesn't necessarily mean spending a large amount of money. End each date by praying God's best for your girl.

1. Go see a play or Christian concert together.
2. Eat out someplace unusual—some place you never have been.
3. Browse around a teen clothing store. Let her show you the kinds of clothes she likes (and doesn't like).
4. Take her to ride go-carts at an amusement park.
5. Go horseback riding.
6. Volunteer together at a nursing home, church, Habitat for Humanity, and so forth.
7. Go on a mission trip together.
8. Go to breakfast together on Saturday morning.
9. Take your dog(s) on a walk together. If you don't own dogs, you can still walk together!

10. Pick her up from school and take her out to lunch. (Check with school administration first.)

11. Go to a coffee shop together.

12. Cook dinner together, letting her choose the menu and help shop for the ingredients.

13. Play Frisbee® in the park.

14. Go get ice cream together.

15. Watch a movie together at a theater.

16. Shop for your wife's birthday or Christmas present.

17. Borrow a friend's telescope and look at the stars on a clear night.

18. Go to a sporting event you both enjoy. Remember, however, to focus on your daughter, not the game!

19. Buy her flowers on special occasions (birthday, opening of a play, soccer championship).

20. Ride bicycles together.

21. Rent an old movie to watch on a rainy afternoon.

22. Create a family Web site together. Gather pictures and stories about your family to post for other family members or friends.

23. Browse through a music store. Ask her to show you her favorite groups and listen to sample songs. Let her listen to some of your favorites.

24. Make a snowman.

25. Play miniature golf.

26. Go bowling. Invite other dads and their daughters to come along.

27. Visit an elderly person in your church who craves company.

28. Go rock-climbing together at an indoor facility. Check the Internet for the one closest to you.

29. Go water skiing or snow skiing.

30. Go to a museum.

A Mother's Journal

A Mother's Journal

CHAPTER 7

Girl Politics

WHILE REMINISCING WITH OLD FRIENDS at my 20-year high school reunion, a classmate, much to my embarrassment, made comments about how mean I had been in junior high school. She recanted in detail things I had said behind her back and times when I had purposely left her out and rallied other girls to do the same. Even though her tone was lighthearted and her words laced with laughter, I found it disturbing that I had earned a spot in the annals of the history of her middle school years as one of the "mean girls." I apologized profusely for my past behavior and chalked it up to the standard adolescent insecurities.

Girls who are "sugar and spice and everything nice" are made, not born. As important as it is to invest time and effort in training our daughters in vital life skills in their early years, it is equally important to train them in relationship skills that will lend to their emotional well-being in the adolescent years.

Anyone who doubts that the inclinations of the heart are evil from childhood, as Genesis 8:21 says, need only attend a junior-high sleepover where an uneven number of girls are present. Gossip, tears, and backbiting make for full-fledged drama, popcorn included. For many girls, the drama begins before middle school; and many moms are caught off guard as they find themselves ill equipped to deal with the sudden onslaught of emotions. Let's face it, many of us are still licking the wounds we sustained on the battlefield of adolescent girl politics. While it is an unfortunate, though normal, part of growing up, we mothers need to play an active role in equipping our daughters with biblical principles to help them navigate the minefield.

Girls who are "sugar and spice and everything nice" are made, not born. As important as it is to invest time and effort in training our daughters in vital life skills in their early years, it is equally important to train them in relationship skills that will lend to their emotional well-being in the adolescent years. And you thought potty training was hard! Add hormones and the standard mother-daughter tensions into the mix (mom has officially reached "dork" status), and it could be one of your biggest challenges in motherhood. Even if your daughter reminds you on a daily basis of how "uncool" you are, do not dismay. She may roll her eyes in response to your words of wisdom, but chances are, she is listening.

The upside to the adolescent years (yes, there is one) is that it provides our daughters with a practice field for developing basic relationship principles. Even though they will make mistakes along the way, they will find themselves better prepared when it comes to future relationships such as marriage and parenting. Often we invest time into our children's education so that they may someday become a productive member of society. We encourage them to pursue extracurricular activities in order to use their talents and teach them teamwork and a sense of accomplishment. However, of what benefit is a degree, a good job, and bookshelves full of awards and trophies if our daughters fail in their relationships with others? With equal devotion we must invest time and effort into training them in basic relationship principles.

Fortunately, we don't have to wing it. Everything we need to raise our daughters to be "sugar and spice and everything nice" and to survive the girls who are "not so nice" can be found in God's Word. Let's take a look at common issues our daughters will most likely face in the precarious adolescent years.

Cliques

If you ask a sampling of mothers with adolescent daughters to say the first word that comes to mind when they hear the phrase "middle school girls," chances are high that a good number will say "cliques." A clique is defined as "a narrow circle of persons associated by common interests or for the accomplishment of a common purpose." The definition goes on to state that it is generally used in a negative sense.

What cliques (different groupings of people, especially girls) existed when you were in junior high and high school?

Did you tend to gravitate to a specific group of girls in your adolescence? If so, which ones? Why?

Did your group of girls exclude others or do things to make others feel inferior? If so, what did you do? What was the result?

Were you ever on the outside of a clique? If so, how did it feel?

What things did you do in order to fit in and be accepted, even if it was negative behavior?

One of the biggest needs among adolescents is to fit in. So strong is this desire that it has led good kids to join gangs or religious cults with wacky beliefs. We should not minimize our daughters' need to fit in, and we should recognize that it is rooted in a desire to be accepted. Girls are, by nature, relational; therefore, they are often drawn to cliques as a means to validate their worth. Our daughters need to be reminded that their true worth is not based on whether they are accepted by others; their true identity is in Christ. Girls who accept that their "worth = who they are in Christ" are less likely to be a part of a clique because they do not feel a need to conform to the expectations of others. In addition, we should assist our daughters in choosing friends who share common interests and hold to the same values and beliefs.

Read the following Scriptures. Paraphrase them and indicate how each applies to cliques.

Psalm 1:1 _____

_____

Proverbs 2:20_____

_____

Luke 6:32-33 _____

_____

1 Corinthians 15:33_____

_____

James 2:1-4_____

_____

_____

I have given my daughter basic information regarding cliques and have warned her of the dangers of such groups. I have told her that a clique is any group that purposely excludes others and acts superior to everyone else. I have also educated her as to the anatomy of a clique. The average clique usually includes one to two strong-willed girls who are the ringleaders and a number of other girls who are the followers. I have warned her that many sweet girls are lured into cliques because they have falsely defined their worth and base their worth on the superficial acceptance of the group. Of course, no clique is complete without one or more targeted victims. Woe to the poor girls who unwillingly become the designated victims.

I think it's important to make a distinction between a clique and a group of girlfriends. A peer group does not constitute a clique. We should encourage our daughters to be nice to everyone, but it is unreasonable to expect that every girl will be in the same group of girlfriends. Just as we have natural preferences when it comes to developing friendships, our daughters, too, will prefer the company of some girls over others because of shared similarities. In the grade-school years, I made an effort to invite all the girls in my daughter's class to her birthday parties, but as she progressed to middle school, we trimmed down the list to a few close friends. I have told my daughter that there is nothing wrong with preferring the company of certain girls over others, but I also cautioned her to be careful that she and her friends do not allow their peer group to transition into a clique that seeks to exclude others.

What can mothers do to steer their daughters away from damaging friendships? Know who your daughter's friends are and do not hesitate to draw boundaries in her friendships. If you see warning signs that indicate your daughter is in an unhealthy friendship or is part of a clique, take a tough stand and, depending on the severity of the situation, either forbid her from continuing the friendship or limit her time with the friends in question. In the end, protecting her character is more important than allowing her to continue in an unhealthy relationship that could produce devastating fallout in the months or years to come.

I recall a girl in high school who was always on the fringe of my peer group. I was in the esteemed "popular group," and at times, it bordered on being a clique. She was a nice and somewhat quiet girl who could have easily found other friends had she been willing to look outside our group. She had somehow rationalized, as many girls do, that acceptance into the popular group would satisfy her longing for worth and value. Even sadder was the fact that it was equally important to her parents that she find her place in the popular group. Week after week she would call girls in the group and invite them to spend the night, often at the prompting of her parents. It seemed that the harder she tried, the meaner we got. How sad that her precious high school years were wasted trying to be friends with girls who did not appreciate or respect her but rather saw her as an annoyance. She deserved so much better, but unfortunately her parents had falsely perceived that "better" was the popular group. Had they seen our résumés, they might have steered her in another direction!

Now that I am a Christian, I feel deep remorse over any part I may have played in hurting her. I can't help but wonder if her parents have ever owned the fact that they, too, played a part in hurting her. As mothers, we must encourage our daughters to "follow the way of good people, and keep to the paths of the righteous" (Prov. 2:20). We must encourage them to treat others with respect and dignity, even if those people aren't a part of the "in" crowd (whatever that crowd might be).

One way we can encourage our daughters in forming healthy relationships that do not exclude others is by setting the example. Unfortunately, cliques do not magically disappear when the graduation tassel is removed. Women continue to form cliques well beyond high school and college. Sadly, some of the most ungodly cliques formed take place within the church.

As an adult, how have you been guilty of being in a clique—even at church?

Is there someone to whom you need to go and ask forgiveness for excluding her?

Our daughters need to understand that cliques are not reserved only for the lunchroom or the cheer squad. They are formed in the fellowship committee at church, in the break room at work, and on the PTA committee at school. As mothers, we bear the responsibility of modeling for our daughters the importance of valuing and including others, even if we may not necessarily choose them to be our closest friends.

Gossip

Years ago, a friend of mine was deeply wounded when she discovered that her best friend had betrayed her trust and shared confidential information related to problems she had experienced in her marriage. Proverbs

16:28 accurately predicted the outcome: "a gossip separates friends." The fallout was devastating and brought an end to a longtime friendship. Both women are Christians, yet the sad story proves that in spite of numerous warnings in Scripture regarding gossip, many women fail to heed the warnings and succumb to the temptation to trade choice verbal morsels.

Gossip has often been treated in the church as a "little" sin, but in Romans 1:29-31, it is listed among such serious sins as unrighteousness, greed, wickedness, envy, murder, deceit, and malice, hating God, arrogance, pride, boastful, and inventing evil. Ouch. Clearly God views gossip as a serious matter. Unfortunately our culture not only condones gossip but also encourages it. Many teen girls' fashion magazines feature columns on celebrity gossip and treat gossip as a standard aspect of life for girls. In a culture that embraces moral relativity, where each person determines what is right and wrong, gossip for most people is barely a blip on the radar screen of "wrong" behaviors. Because of this, our daughters can expect some ribbing from friends if they take a stand against gossip on the ground that it is wrong. As mothers, we need to remind them that they are set apart from the world and that gossip is a sin. Scripture warns of the dangers of the untamed tongue.

Following are Bible verses that deal directly with gossip or misuse of the tongue. Read each of them and match them to the truth they proclaim.

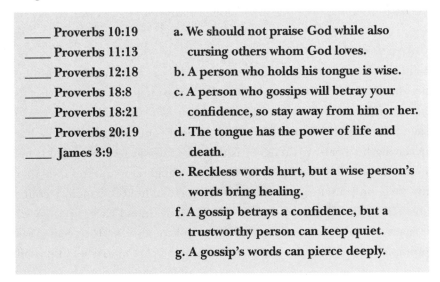

____ Proverbs 10:19	a. We should not praise God while also cursing others whom God loves.
____ Proverbs 11:13	b. A person who holds his tongue is wise.
____ Proverbs 12:18	c. A person who gossips will betray your confidence, so stay away from him or her.
____ Proverbs 18:8	d. The tongue has the power of life and death.
____ Proverbs 18:21	e. Reckless words hurt, but a wise person's words bring healing.
____ Proverbs 20:19	f. A gossip betrays a confidence, but a trustworthy person can keep quiet.
____ James 3:9	g. A gossip's words can pierce deeply.

These verses are good to discuss with your daughter. I have gently encouraged my daughter to consider posting some of the verses by our computer as a reminder when she is sending instant messages back and forth with her friends. Chatting with friends online can easily become a breeding ground for swapping the latest gossip. In fact, my daughter has been sent instant messages that contain comments that were shared in confidence by another girl to the sender. It is common practice for girls to cut and paste comments and send them on to others. I have told my daughter that this is no different from the old-fashioned version of swapping gossip by secret telling or passing notes and have encouraged her to take a stand when someone sends gossip her way. While the computer may act as a buffer or make it appear less harmful, the effects are just as damaging.

Interestingly, the word used for gossip in the King James Version is *whisperer*. When I think of whisperer, I think of the game of gossip, where you pass a phrase around a circle of people by whispering it. Of course, when the last person states what she heard, it is usually not remotely close to the original phrase. The end result of real-life gossip is no different. Our daughters should be on guard for phrases that start with "Did you hear . . ." or "I probably shouldn't say this . . ." If they offer a gentle response that heads off gossip, it won't take long for other girls to figure out that they are not a willing party when it comes to gossip. I have told my daughter that if she finds herself on the receiving end of gossip on a regular basis, then the ones passing it along clearly see her as a willing party.

Our Example

I am convicted by the fact that no matter how diligent I am in training my daughter to resist participating in gossip, if I model otherwise to her when it comes to my own life, my words will ring hollow. James 1:26 says, "If anyone thinks he is religious, without controlling his tongue but deceiving his heart, his religion is useless." I would be devastated if my failure to practice what I preach caused my daughter to question whether my "religion is useless." No doubt, it is a verse to hold this mom accountable! To err is human, and I often blow it. Many times I have experienced conviction from God over words I have spoken, and the Holy Spirit has prompted me to make it right by contacting the person to whom I passed along forbidden morsels and asking forgiveness. This is a painful exercise, but it makes me think twice the next time I am tempted to gossip. If my daughter witnesses me partaking in gossip, it is my responsibility to own my sin, tell her I was wrong, and ask her forgiveness. {125}

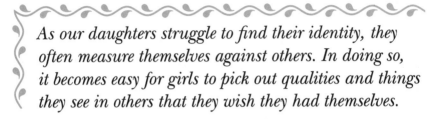

As our daughters struggle to find their identity, they often measure themselves against others. In doing so, it becomes easy for girls to pick out qualities and things they see in others that they wish they had themselves.

Jealousy

Beware of the big green monster called "jealousy." If your daughter has reached the middle-school years, you have most likely encountered this monster. By high school it has usually morphed into the Loch Ness monster. As our daughters struggle to find their identity, they often measure themselves against others. In doing so, it becomes easy for girls to pick out qualities and things they see in others that they wish they had themselves. We mothers can certainly relate to the temptation to want someone else's dress size, another's income, another's house, car, personality, obedient children, romantic husband, and so on and so on. Our daughters are no different. Let's see what Scripture has to say about being envious.

Read Exodus 20:17.
What is the relationship between coveting and being jealous?

Why do you think God included this in the Ten Commandments?

Read Proverbs 14:30.
What is the warning in this verse? What does it mean?

Read 1 Corinthians 13:4.
Why is love not compatible with envy?

Read 1 Timothy 6:6-10.
According to Paul, what is "great gain"?

How did we enter the world? How will we leave it? Why is this important?

What is the consequence of trying to amass wealth and possessions?

How can the love of money be a root of all kinds of evil? How have you seen jealousy over money or material possessions result in evil?

How can envy bring grief?

When you were a teenager, what made you jealous?

What areas of jealousy do you struggle with the most as an adult?
Check the ones that apply to you.

☐ house	☐ romantic husband
☐ car	☐ physical beauty
☐ body shape	☐ intellect
☐ personality	☐ vacations
☐ job	☐ community status
☐ clothes	☐ family
☐ speaking ability	☐ bank account
☐ popularity	☐ sense of humor
☐ singing ability	☐ children's accomplishments

We can help our daughters avoid the bite of the big green monster by reminding them that they are unique creations of God and that He has equipped them with unique talents and abilities to be used for His good and glory. As they come to believe in the person God created them to be, the longing to be like someone else will dissipate. Unfortunately, many adult women fail to reach this point. For the mothers who have not learned this truth, it will be impossible to pass this truth along to their daughters. Jealousy is one of many manifestations of a girl's (or woman's) mistakenly defined worth. A true mark of properly defined worth is the ability to take joy in the attributes and achievements of others. Rare is the woman who is comfortable enough with who she is so that she can sincerely rejoice with another woman who accomplishes or attains something that she had wanted for herself.

As I mentioned in an earlier chapter, I remember vividly a personal encounter I had with jealousy in the seventh grade. It was the beginning of the school year, and cheerleading elections were being held. Nearly one hundred girls signed up to try out in front of a panel of judges. The judges would pick 15 girls who would then try out in front of the student body to determine who would fill the six coveted spots. My life goal at that point was to be a cheerleader. My best friend and I had been practicing cheers and holding mock tryouts since fifth grade. Her older sister was a cheerleader, and when I saw her in her uniform, I knew it was my destiny. If you're from Texas, you understand—cheerleading rules!

Everyone thought I would make it because I had two things going for me: back handsprings and popularity. I was confident that my skills would get me past the judges and my popularity would earn me the student vote. Unfortunately, the script did not play out according to plan. I will never forget sitting on the gym floor among the multitude of seventh-grade girls as the cheerleading sponsor read the names of the 15 girls who had made it past the judges. I waited and waited to hear my name, but when the last name was called, my name was not among the 15. My best friend had made it past the judges, but I had not. I was devastated. Never had I imagined the story would turn out that way. I was overcome with jealousy, and when it came time for the student body vote, I could hardly stand to see my best friend up on stage realizing my dream. Rather than rejoice with her, I was focused on myself and consumed with envy. When it came time to circle six names on the ballot, I did not circle her name.

{ 128 }

All the same, she made the squad, and I feigned the obligatory excitement. In the months that followed, it cut me to the core to see her in the uniform and cheering at the games. We used to walk home from school together, but now she had to stay after school for practice. I would walk home alone, sulking over my status as a noncheerleader. The next year we both made the squad, and her genuine excitement for me made it all the worse when I reflected back on my shameful actions the year before.

As mothers, we should help our daughters process moments of disappointment before they transition into jealousy. As they come to realize that God does not play favorites and has a unique plan and purpose for each person, it will free them up to rejoice with others. When they learn to be content with the gifts and talents God has given them, they will be able to enjoy the talents and gifts He has given others. More importantly, as they witness mothers who are content with themselves, content with their circumstances, and sincerely content when others prosper, they will take notice.

When it comes to raising girls who are "sugar and spice and everything nice," there is no secret formula. We can do our part by equipping them with biblical truths, setting boundaries, and encouraging them to take the high road in difficult situations. In the end, it will be up to our daughters to determine whether they choose nice or not so nice. As a past middle-school, not-so-nice girl, my prayer for my daughter is that she will be remembered at her 20-year high school reunion as one of the "nice girls" who reflected the love of Christ to others.

TALKING POINTS

1. Discuss a time when you felt excluded from a clique in your teen years. Share how you felt and how you dealt with the rejection. If you were involved in a clique, talk about any regret you have felt over treating others poorly.

2. Ask your daughter about the different cliques or groups in her school, especially within her own peer group.

3. Talk together about the difference between sharing information about someone (Example: Sara broke her arm at cheerleading practice) and gossip. Commit together to refrain from gossiping.

4. Talk about the things teen girls tend to get jealous about. Also share times when you've struggled with envy as an adult.

A Mother's Journal

A Mother's Journal

Leaving a Heritage

Jesus told a parable about two people who built houses. One person built his house on sand; so when the wind and rain came, the house had no foundation to withstand the storm. It fell with a great crash. The other man built his sand on rock, and that house stood despite the forces that came against it.

If our daughters do not learn to build their lives on something stronger than the sandy foundation of today's culture, they have no chance when the storms of life blow. They must learn to build on the rock—on a relationship with God. They must learn that God's Word, faith, and prayer are essential ingredients in weathering the hurricanes they will face. As mothers, you and I play a critical role in guiding our daughters to build their lives on these sure pillars. In this chapter, we will focus on two of these pillars—prayer and faith. (The DVD available with this book contains a segment that discusses leaving a heritage of God's Word.)

They must learn to build on the rock—on a relationship with God. They must learn that God's Word, faith, and prayer are essential ingredients in weathering the hurricanes they will face.

The Heritage of Prayer

Prayer, simply put, is conversing with God. The more our daughters talk with God, the more in touch they will be with His intended purpose for their lives. A consistent prayer life can act as a safeguard against mediocrity and a tendency toward a lukewarm Christian faith. Well-balanced conversations with God include both talking to God and listening to Him. After all, how good would a relationship with a friend be if our conversations always boiled down to a long to-do list for the other person?

Listed below are several Scriptures. Read each and record what they tell you about prayer.

Psalm 55:22: _____

_____

_____

Psalm 62:8: _____

_____

_____

Matthew 7:7-11: _____

_____

_____

Philippians 4:6-7: _____

_____

_____

_____

The ACTS Model

One of the simplest and best prayer models I have found that leads to a well-balanced prayer life is the ACTS model. ACTS is an acronym that stands for Adoration (or praise), Confession, Thanksgiving, and Supplication (making requests of God for others or ourselves). My husband and I have diligently taught the ACTS model to our children and have used it as part of their bedtime ritual. We found the ACTS model to be user-friendly for our children even when they were young. The goal is that as our children get older, they will take the initiative to reach for His hand on a regular basis.

ADORATION

It seems only fitting that prayer to the Holy God should begin with acknowledgment of His divine characteristics and attributes. Our rela- tionship with God is put into the proper perspective when we, the creation, submit in awe and reverence to our Creator. It is an expression of faith when we take the focus off our own needs and direct our attention to the One who promises to meet our needs. If it is difficult for you to voice your adoration to God, you can praise Him using Scripture. Nothing is more beautiful than praying Scripture aloud to God in the form of praise.

CONFESSION

The C of ACTS stands for confession. Confession is basically agreeing with God concerning our sin and feeling sorrow for our sin. Unless we think and feel the same way that God does about our sin, we will not repent (turn from our sin and turn back to God). (See 2 Cor. 7:10.) During the confession part of prayer time with my children, I encourage them to think of something specific they may have done that day, rather than make a general sweeping statement (Example: "Lord, I confess that I was wrong when I spoke disrespectfully to my mom when she picked me up late from school" versus "Lord, I confess that I can be disrespectful to my parents"). If their confession involves a wrongdoing against another person, encourage them to make it right with the person by asking for forgiveness. If you are taking turns going back and forth with the ACTS model, allow your daughter to hear you confess some specific sin that you committed that day. In doing so, you model to your daughter that we all (yes, even moms!) have sinned and fall short of the glory of God. (See Rom. 3:23.) Once your daughter becomes a Christian, encourage her to take an inventory of her day and respond to conviction that the Holy Spirit may have placed upon her heart. She may not always feel comfortable confessing her sins in your presence, so encourage her to continue her confession time alone after your prayer time together has ended.

When our daughters confess their sins on a daily basis and acknowledge God's forgiveness, it reminds them that sin is a serious matter. In a world of moral relativism, the discipline of confession will remind our daughters that there are absolute moral standards that dictate right and wrong, good and evil. However, we should be quick to assure our daughters that no sin is too big for the forgiveness of God. (See 1 John 1:9).

THANKSGIVING

The T in ACTS stands for "thanksgiving." When I think of thanking God, I am reminded of the 10 lepers in Luke 17:12-18. They all cried out to Jesus to have pity on them and heal them. He responded to their cries and told them to "go and show yourselves to the priests" (v. 14), and then He healed them on their way. Only one bothered to return and thank Him. Jesus asked the man, "Were not 10 cleansed? Where are the nine? Didn't any return to give glory to God except this foreigner? (vv. 17-18). Oftentimes, I am guilty, like the nine lepers, of failing to thank God for answered prayers.

One solution to this problem is to use a prayer journal. In a blank notebook, divide the pages into two columns. In one column, list your prayer requests; in the other column, mark when and how the prayer was answered. When keeping a prayer journal, we are more likely to notice when God answers our prayers and offer Him the thanks He deserves.

God reminds us in Psalm 50:23 that "whoever sacrifices a thank offerings honors Me." In addition to teaching our daughters to thank God for answered prayer, we should also teach them to express thanks for things they might otherwise take for granted. This include the blessings of family, extended family, church family, a place to live, food to eat, freedom to worship; the list goes on and on. If our daughters hear us express thanks to God for our many blessings, we model having a heart of gratitude.

SUPPLICATION

The S in ACTS stands for "supplication." Supplication is when we submit our requests or petitions to God on behalf of ourselves or others. As a reflection of the principle of putting others before ourselves, I am trying to develop the habit of submitting requests for others before I pray for myself. I have taught the same principle to my daughter.

We must teach our daughters early on that God is the Father of compassion and the God of all comfort, who is capable of comforting them in all their troubles. (See 2 Cor. 1:3-4.) "Troubles" can range from an "owie" when they're 2, being left off the invitation list for a big party when they're 10, a breakup when they are 17, or anything else that leads to tears or a broken heart. As much as we desire to protect our daughters from hurtful situations in life, we cannot do the impossible. While we should rejoice if our daughters count us as trusted confidants when they are hurting, we need to be careful to show them comfort while at the same time pointing them to the only One who can mend a broken heart.

We must also teach our daughters to submit to God's authority when we pray. Submission to God expressed through prayer says, "Your will be done," even if it is an answer that was not expected. If our daughters understand this concept, they will be less likely to question why God may choose not to answer some of their prayers in the ways that they hope. They will understand that "no" or "wait" is as valid an answer to their prayers as "yes."

We must teach our daughters that God is accessible every minute of every day and wants us to come to Him.

Pray Without Ceasing

When I was a new believer, I remember experiencing some confusion over the call in 1 Thessalonians 5:17 to "pray without ceasing" (KJV). How does one pray constantly? The Greek word used for "without ceasing," is *adialeiptos,* which means "uninterruptedly." Since prayer is the way we communicate with God, and communicating with God is critical to our living as God desires, it only makes sense that we should be mindful of anything that would interrupt our communication with God. While I believe it is important to have a set time for prayer, it does not have to be relegated to that time only. We must teach our daughters that God is accessible every minute of every day and wants us to come to Him. When they develop the instinct to turn to God throughout their day, whether to lift up a request or a praise to Him, they will learn the art of what it is to pray without ceasing. Children who develop the habit of talking to God throughout each day on their own initiative are much less likely to fall into tempting situations or make foolish decisions when standing at the crossroads of a difficult choice.

Prayer is a dialogue with God. We speak to Him, and He also speaks to us if we're willing to be quiet and listen. One of the most difficult things for me when it comes to prayer is learning to stop and listen for the still, quiet voice of God. Sometimes in my morning prayer time, I spend moments in silence after going through the ACTS model. I've been amazed at the answers I have received when I've stopped talking to God and started listening to Him. I have encouraged my daughter to take time to listen carefully for God's voice.

Praying for Our Daughters

While this section has focused on equipping our daughters with a heritage of prayer, it is equally important for us to exercise the privilege of praying for our daughters. Entire books have been devoted to the subject of mothers praying for their children. My husband and I consistently tell our children that we are praying for them. My husband has made it part of his morning routine to pray with and for my children at breakfast. He briefly describes character attributes that our children need to develop, and he prays for that attribute to be developed in their lives. He has been doing it for so long that my children can define the meaning of each attribute before my husband finishes reading the definition. If you don't have a list of character attributes that you define and pray with your children, consider using the one below. You can pray for a different character trait each day of the month.

31 Christian Attributes to Pray for Our Children

1. Pray for a spirit of humility. —James 4:10
2. Pray for a spirit of reverence. —Proverbs 9:10
3. Pray for a spirit of purity. —Matthew 5:8
4. Pray for a spirit of purpose. —Proverbs 4:25
5. Pray for a spirit of simplicity. —Romans 12:8
6. Pray for a spirit of commitment. —Joshua 24:15
7. Pray for a spirit of diligence. —2 Peter 1:5
8. Pray for a spirit of servanthood. —Galatians 6:9-10

9. Pray for a spirit of consistency. —James 1:8

10. Pray for a spirit of assurance. —Hebrews 10:22

11. Pray for a spirit of availability. —Isaiah 6:8

12. Pray for a spirit of loyalty. —Ruth 1:16

13. Pray for a spirit of sensitivity. —Luke 10:30-37

14. Pray for a spirit of compassion. —Mark 8:1-2

15. Pray for a spirit of tenderness. —2 Kings 22:19

16. Pray for a spirit of maturity. —Hebrews 5:12-14

17. Pray for a spirit of holiness. —1 Peter 1:16

18. Pray for a spirit of reliability. —1 Corinthians 4:2

19. Pray for a spirit of revelation. —Ephesians 1:15-18

20. Pray for a spirit of denial. —Luke 9:23

21. Pray for a spirit of confidence. —Philippians 4:13

22. Pray for a spirit of integrity. —Romans 12:17

23. Pray for a spirit of repentance. —Luke 3:8

24. Pray for a spirit of trust. —Psalm 125:1

25. Pray for a spirit of submission. —Ephesians 5:21

26. Pray for a spirit of teachability. —Titus 3:2

27. Pray for a spirit of prayer. —Isaiah 40:31

28. Pray for a spirit of unity. —1 Corinthians 1:10

29. Pray for a spirit of restoration. —Isaiah 61:1-2

30. Pray for a spirit of authority. —Matthew 16:19

31. Pray for a spirit of generosity. —Matthew 10:8

I realize that some mothers who are reading this may be experiencing a strained relationship with their daughters. If this is the case for you, suggest to your daughter that you pray aloud with her and for her once a week. Allow her to hear you thank God for her.

A dear friend of mine once mentioned in a speaking engagement that she developed the habit of praying for each of her children out loud in their respective rooms while they were at school. The first time I tried it, I ended up carrying a box of tissues with me from room to room. The experience moved me beyond words. Someday, God willing, they too might stand in their children's bedrooms, tissues in hand, and verbally beseech the loving Father on behalf of their own children.

A Heritage of Faith

One of the most important things we can leave our daughters is a heritage of faith. Probably the biggest determinant in whether we leave our daughters a heritage of faith is whether we, as mothers, model to them what having faith in Jesus looks like. One of my favorite definitions of *faith* is "belief in action." It is one thing to verbalize our belief in Christ to our daughters but quite another to act on that belief. If a mother's actions and attitudes consistently contradict her expressed belief in Jesus, her daughter will receive a mixed message that faith in Christ is all talk and no action.

Are you modeling a sincere faith in Christ to your daughter? Are your actions and attitudes consistent with your expressed belief in Jesus? If not, your daughter could be left with the impression that faith in Christ is not a serious matter. Below are 10 faith compromisers, which, if practiced consistently and modeled to your daughter, will prevent you from leaving her a true heritage of faith in Christ.

Top 10 Faith Compromisers

1. NOT ATTENDING CHURCH REGULARLY

Consistent attendance at a Bible-believing church is essential for spiritual growth. Why is this important? In a Bible-believing church, Christians learn the Bible and how to apply it to their lives; have an opportunity to fellowship with other believers; participate in corporate worship; and receive encouragement, accountability, and comfort.

Years ago, when I was a Sunday School teacher in the children's area, my heart was grieved over the children on my class roster who attended Sunday School and church only sporadically. While sporadic attendance was better than no attendance at all, the moms' and/or dads' unwillingness to make Sunday School and church a priority sent the clear message to their children that Sunday School and church attendance was not important. I also grieved over the parents who told me they stopped attending Sunday School or church because one or more of their children did not want to go. Given that logic, I wonder if they let their children miss school on days they would rather sleep in or watch their favorite cartoon.

The spiritual foundation established by consistent church attendance will lend itself to a stronger and deeper faith in Jesus. We rarely allow our children to have friends spend the night on Saturday nights or spend the night out with friends on Saturday night. We make occasional exceptions if the friend they wish to invite over does not attend church. On the rare occasions where they are allowed to spend the night out on Saturday nights, we expect them to go to bed at a reasonable hour and attend church the next morning with their friend. There is no reason that God should get the dregs of our lives on Sunday morning. He deserves our full attention, energy, and devotion. Just as we desire that our children go to bed at a reasonable hour on school nights so they are rested the next day, we should expect the same on "church nights" so they will be rested for Sunday School and church.

> *True worshipers submit to the will and authority of God on a continual, daily basis. Worship is love for God expressed through consistent obedience. It will be impossible to offer ourselves to God as "living sacrifices" without obedience.*

2. WORSHIPING ONLY ON SUNDAYS

Many Christians mistakenly assume that "worship" means only singing hymns or choruses on Sunday morning at church. In truth, Scripture tells us that worship is much more than that.

Romans 12:1 tells us, "I urge you to present your bodies as a living sacrifice, holy and pleasing to God; this is your spiritual worship." It is God's desire that we offer ourselves to Him in worship on a continual basis rather than one morning a week. Worship is a state of mind that acknowledges God as holy and worthy of awe and reverence. Such an attitude overflows into our actions every day, not just our posture on Sunday morning. It's important to worship God corporately each Sunday, but it is equally important to live a life of worship every day of the week. True worshipers submit to the will and authority of God on a continual, daily basis. Worship is love for God expressed through consistent obedience. It will be impossible to offer ourselves to God as "living sacrifices" without obedience.

3. WORRYING OR FAILING TO TRUST GOD IN TIMES OF ADVERSITY

There is no greater peace in life than coming to a place where you can say, "Whatever, Lord. Your will be done." I am ashamed to say that in my nearly 20-year walk with Christ, I have spent most of those years in the freak-out mode when adversity hits. I had always admired Christians who appeared calm while in the eye of the storm and wondered if, perhaps, they didn't curl up in a fetal position behind closed doors. As I became more devoted to knowing God through His Word and prayer, I began to put my belief in Him into action. It is not that I don't experience an occasional moment of panic in times of uncertainty, but I can usually renew my mind in the truth that has become embedded within my heart, which helps extinguish the onset of doubt.

Whether it is a loss of a job, a prodigal child gone astray, a broken marriage, or a child months shy of getting her driver's license, we can cast our cares on the Lord and He will sustain us. (See Ps. 55:22.) When we respond with worry, distrust God consistently, and model that lack of trust before our daughters, they will learn that our actions don't match our beliefs. When we can pour our hearts out before God in confident trust, we leave a strong example for our children to follow.

4. FAILING TO PUT YOUR MONEY WHERE YOUR MOUTH IS

A survey found that only six percent of born-again Christian households tithed to their churches in 2002.[1] But what does God's Word tell us about our giving to God? Malachi 3:10 instructs believers to "bring the full 10 percent into the storehouse so that there may be food in My house." A tithe is one-tenth of our earnings. In giving back to God, we acknowledge that all we have belongs to God; without Him we would have nothing.

Why is a failure to tithe a faith compromiser? If one claims to believe wholeheartedly in Christ and the commandments set forth in God's Word, then that believer should be willing to entrust to God a portion (10 percent or more) of what rightly belongs to Him in the first place. Regardless of whether a Christian's failure to tithe is due to a real or perceived lack of finances or simply a preference to spend the money elsewhere, failure to tithe shows a lack of trust in God. Those who cannot trust God with their finances will struggle to trust Him in other areas of life as well.

I have told my daughter that she should not even consider marrying a man who compromises in the area of tithing. In doing so, he shows a lack of faith in God that will not be limited to his finances. If he can dismiss God's command to tithe when it becomes difficult to do so, what keeps him from dismissing the command to remain faithful in marriage whenever the marriage gets difficult? {143}

5. BEING A WHINER

If you want to send a mixed message to your daughter, tell her that she can have an abundant and content life if she will allow Jesus to be the Lord of her life—but then whine and complain in front of her all the time. If you want your daughter to adopt your Christian faith and experience the abundant life that Christ referred to in John 10:10, she must see that your faith in Christ has resulted in the abundant life. Faith in Christ should bring a new attitude fueled by an overwhelming sense of gratefulness to Him. No doubt, we all experience a good whine from time to time. The problem arises if we are chronic whiners. Chronic whiners can hardly carry on a conversation without saying something negative or critical.

The root of whining is discontentment, and discontentment is always a choice. The root of discontentment is ungratefulness to, and lack of faith in, God. If you find yourself being discontent, a practical way to address it is to make a mental or physical list of all you have to be thankful for. Our daughters are watching and listening. If we are whining mothers, we will almost certainly raise whining daughters, who will someday grow up to be whining mothers. We need to teach our daughters that too much "whine" can be hazardous to their spiritual health.

6. NOT SHARING YOUR FAITH WITH OTHERS

A person's final words are always of importance. In Jesus' final words before He ascended, He could have emphasized loving others or giving to the poor, but instead He exhorted believers to "go, therefore, and make disciples of all nations, baptizing them in the name of the Father and of the Son and of the Holy Spirit, teaching them to observe everything I have commanded you" (Matt. 28:19-20). Jesus was not making a mere suggestion to tell others about Him; He was giving a command.

We minimize the importance of faith in Jesus Christ if we teach our daughters that a personal relationship with Jesus is the most important thing in life yet fail to share Him with others. It sends a message that we are concerned only with our own salvation. In 1 Corinthians 9:16, Paul said, "Woe to me if I do not preach the gospel!" As recipients of the life-changing power of the gospel message, we too should be compelled to tell others about the gospel of Jesus. As mothers, we need to teach our daughters this truth by our words and, most importantly, our lifestyles.

{ 1 4 4 }

7. MOLDING YOUR FAITH TO FIT YOUR LIFE

Many Christians treat their faith as an afterthought or minor detail in the scheme of their lives. Their belief in Christ is merely one of many aspects that influence their lives, rather than being the preeminent, foundational aspect of their lives. We all can probably think of times we were shocked when someone told us she was a Christian because her life did not support it. I can't help but think of Peter, who denied Christ three times after declaring to Him, "Even if everyone runs away because of You, I will never run away!" (Matt. 26:33). Peter discovered the hard way that believing in Christ is not always easy. When the rubber hit the road, he chose safety over following Jesus. Peter faced a crisis of belief—was Jesus who He claimed to be? In the end Peter did determine that, indeed, Jesus was the Messiah, the Son of the living God. By the time he proclaimed Christ to thousands on the day of Pentecost, Peter had remolded his life to fit his faith. He was transformed from a "closet Christian" to one of the boldest and most vocal disciples of Christ ever known.

Would those who know you be shocked to discover that you are a Christian? Would people be able to identify you as a faithful follower of Christ after spending time with you? If not, you run the risk of leaving your daughter a heritage of watered-down faith. If this is the case, she may conclude that *Christian* is merely a label rather than a lifestyle. The only way to prevent this is to develop your life around your faith in Jesus rather than attempt to make your faith fit comfortably into your life.

8. FAILING TO PUT YOUR PAST IN ITS PLACE

After years of ministering to women, I have determined that one of the greatest hindrances to women growing into mature, faithful Christians is their failure to put their past in its place. I often tell women in my speaking engagements that Satan's greatest desire is to be granted their souls for all eternity. Once a woman becomes a Christian, she is out of Satan's reach for eternity. At that point he moves to Plan B, in which he will do everything in his power to burden her with shame and false guilt over her past. A failure to understand adequately God's grace and forgiveness will hinder her from sharing the power of the cross with others.

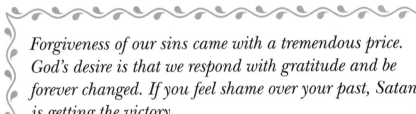

Forgiveness of our sins came with a tremendous price. God's desire is that we respond with gratitude and be forever changed. If you feel shame over your past, Satan is getting the victory.

I know firsthand the toll that shame and guilt over the past can take on your spiritual life. When the skeletons in my closet began to tumble out, I had a hard time believing that God could actually forgive me for some of the things I had done. Somewhere in the midst of my guilt trip, the Holy Spirit convicted my heart that by failing to accept that all my sins had been forgiven, I was minimizing the death of my Savior on the cross. Forgiveness of our sins came with a tremendous price. God's desire is that we respond with gratitude and be forever changed. If you feel shame over your past, Satan is getting the victory.

As much as we desire to protect our daughters from falling into some of the same temptations and sins we may have experienced, it is impossible to keep our thumbs on them every minute of every day. They too will commit sins along the way and find themselves in need of a loving, forgiving Savior. If you are hesitant to share some of your past mistakes with your daughter at times when it would be appropriate, ask yourself why. If you are overwhelmed with shame, it could be that the enemy (Satan) has done a number on you. Don't allow him the opportunity to hold you in bondage to your past any longer. If you have, by faith, received Jesus as your Savior, He has set you free from the spiritual consequences and bondage of your sins. If your daughter witnesses a mother whose heart is overwhelmed with gratitude at the mere thought of the cross, your daughter will have a better understanding of God's grace. She will also know that it came with a heavy price.

{ 146 }

One of the most common questions I get when doing events for mothers and daughters is, "How much do I tell my daughter about my past?" There is no absolute answer to this question, but I tell mothers to spend some time praying about it first. I caution them to check their motives and make sure they are sharing for the right reasons. If they are sharing mistakes from their past to receive comfort from their daughters, they are sharing for the wrong motives. It is inappropriate for us to place a burden on our daughters to meet our emotional needs or to heal our past hurts. Sharing mistakes from our pasts should be for the purpose of illustrating our regret for past sin and the power of God's forgiveness, nothing more. Also, I caution mothers that it should be age appropriate and to avoid specifics if they are led to share. They should avoid sharing details that serve little or no purpose.

9. BEING PRIDEFUL AND LEGALISTIC

One morning, while reading the newspaper, I ran across a story on the front page about several college women from the University of Texas who had modeled nude for an issue of *Playboy* magazine that featured college women from across the country. My heart was saddened when I read that one of the girls was a pastor's daughter, a past member of the Fellowship of Christian Athletes in high school, and had been involved in her church youth group. In the article she claimed that "her faith was no longer important to her."

Out of curiosity I e-mailed her the following day and politely asked her if she would be willing to share with me the factors that led her to conclude that her faith was no longer important. Her response was far from kind, to say the least, but in between her excessive use of profanities, she indicated that her father had been a primary factor. She said that he was harsh, unloving, critical, and legalistic. Nothing she could ever do was good enough in his eyes. She said he knew the Bible backward and forward and had quoted verses to her on a daily basis since the time she was young. In high school she did not drink, smoke, date, or curse, and she attended church every time the doors opened, but she claimed that it still was not enough to satisfy her father. When she got to college, she let {147} loose. It was the classic tale of good girl gone bad. While my gut told me that there was another side to this sad story, I couldn't help but wonder if this young lady's words didn't have a ring of truth to them.

As mothers, we would be wise to remember that rules without relationship equal rebellion. Jesus had harsh words for the Pharisees in Scripture who were legalistic and nitpicked over the letter of the law, using it primarily to pass judgment on everyone but themselves. Worst of all, they did so absent of the love of God. *If I have all faith, so that I can move mountains, but do not have love, I am nothing* (1 Cor. 13:2b).

10. FAILING TO HAVE A DAILY QUIET TIME

It will be impossible to pass down a heritage of faith to our daughters unless we consistently set aside time for prayer and reading God's Word. The more we talk to God in prayer and the more we get to know Him through His Word, the deeper our faith in Him. Daughters who witness mothers who have consistent prayer lives and depend on His Word (the Bible) for their daily sustenance will witness, firsthand, belief in action. Show your daughter the devotional book you use. Talk to her about what you learned in your quiet time today. Ask her to pray for you specifically when an issue arises. Don't assume that she knows you spend time alone with your Savior. Give her glimpses into your devotional life.

Conclusion

Recently, my husband and I were in the market for a small lake cabin. In one weekend alone, we must have looked at a dozen or more homes. Upon entering one of the homes, my realtor informed me that original owner who had lived in the home for some 30 plus years was an elderly man who had passed away. His children were left with the task of selling the home. As we walked through room after room, I couldn't help but notice post-it notes stuck to certain items or pieces of furniture in the home. Upon further inspection, I noticed that each Post-it® note had the name of a person. Apparently, his loved ones had come in and tagged the items that they wanted to keep. It brought to mind Psalms 49:10: "For one can see that wise men die; the foolish and the senseless also pass away. Then they leave their wealth to others." It got me thinking about how we often spend our time and energy gathering up meaningless possessions that someday will likely be tagged with a Post-it® note or dropped off at the nearest Goodwill. I don't know about you, but I sure hope to leave my children, grandchildren, and the generations to follow a richer heritage than random trinkets scattered throughout my home. It is my prayer that they will inherit my heart for prayer, my commitment to spend time in God's Word, or my devotion to Christ. When all is said and done, those are the things worthy of a Post-it® note.

My daughter has been given a great, godly heritage, and so has yours. How do I know that? Because you cared enough to set aside time to do this study, and that speaks volumes about the importance you place on your call as a mother. We as mothers can do our part in passing down the torch of a godly heritage, but in the end, it will be up to our daughters to decide whether they will carry the torch and, in turn, pass it down to their own children. Let us rest in the hope of Proverbs 22:6: "Teach a youth about the way he should go; even when he is old he will not depart from it."

1. Barna Study, *www.barna.org.*

TALKING POINTS

1. Each week after church, take some time as a family to discuss the sermon. Talk about how the sermon impacts each of your lives as individuals and as a family.

2. As a family, discuss ways God has met your needs this week.

3. Ask your daughter about any questions she might have concerning the validity of God's Word. Review the arguments in this chapter for the validity of Scripture. Discuss these with your daughter.

4. The next time a problem comes up, talk about what God's Word says about the issue. This will help your daughter begin to look to God's Word for guidance. It will also help reinforce the truth that God's Word is relevant in today's world.

5. If your family participates in a regular devotional time together, use "31 Christian Attributes to Pray for Our Children" as a guide to pray for your daughter.

A Mother's Journal

A Mother's Journal

Leading a Small-Group Study

Facilitating a small group of women in Bible study or another ministry can be a terrific opportunity to see women grow in the Lord. Here are five tips you can use in your group times to truly facilitate discussion:

1. **Avoid dominating and controlling the group.** The facilitator's role is to draw out other people and encourage them to share. Share your perspective to stimulate discussion when others are reluctant. When discussion is free-flowing, wait until others have shared and adequate time remains for your comments.

2. **Encourage group participation.** If only a few women respond, say, "Let's hear from some of you who have not yet had the opportunity to share." If you sense that a group member would like to share but is hesitant, say: "I sense that you would like to share. Is that the case?" Refrain from putting anyone on the spot by calling on them by name.

3. **Ask simple, clear, open-ended questions.** Open-ended questions often begin with the words *what, how,* or *why.* They allow group members to respond with feelings and ideas that are important to them (for example, "What do you think about ... ?" or "How do you feel about ... ?"). Open-ended questions challenge group members to think and avoid a bias.

4. **Deal with difficult questions honestly.** Be willing to say, "I don't know. Does anyone else have input?" Admit your own humanity and imperfections. Members are more likely to share with a fellow struggler than with someone who gives the impression she knows all the answers. If the answer cannot be found, ask someone to look it up before the next session or offer to do so yourself.

5. **Keep discussion Bible-centered.** Members may disagree on a particular interpretation. It's OK to say, "Here's what I believe." "We may agree to disagree." But as facilitator, don't let "anything go." Refer back to the Scripture.

This article was adapted from a chapter in *Transformed Lives: Taking Women's Ministry to the Next Level.* © Copyright 2000. LifeWay Christian Resources. Used by permission.

SESSION 1

The Choice Before You

Supplies and Resources
- Name tags
- Large note cards or sheets of paper
- Masking tape
- Felt-tip markers
- Post-it® notes (2 colors)
- Pens
- Bibles
- Poster board (optional)
- TV/DVD player

Introduction

As women arrive, direct them to a table where they will make a name tag for themselves and a name sign for their daughter(s). The name signs should be large enough to be placed on a wall, preferably where they will remain throughout the study. Direct women to place the name signs on the designated wall. Signs can overlap randomly without a pattern or trying to line them up. Just make sure names can be read from a distance. If you cannot leave the names on a focal wall for the entire study, place on the wall a large poster board. In large letters with a felt-tip marker, write the words, *Our Girls.* Provide markers in a variety of colors and direct the women to write the names of their daughters on the poster board. You can then take down the name poster after each session and put it back up the following week.

When women have completed these two tasks, direct them to small groups of chairs you have arranged. Direct them to introduce themselves to the other women in the group and to share stories of the birth of their daughters and favorite memories of their daughters as children.

Cultural Concerns

Note the names of the daughters on the wall. Point out that the women in the room have in common their love and concern for their daughters and a desire to be godly mothers who help their daughters move through adolescence having fun, being safe, and discovering who God wants them to be. Also point out that teen girls must deal with a lot of issues. Some are common for teenagers over time; some are new or more threatening in this generation. As a reference, discuss some statistics from the introduction.

Distribute pens and pads of Post-it notes® (all one color). Invite each woman to take three to five notes and to write one cultural concern on each piece of paper. Direct the women to go to the wall of names and to randomly place the Post-it® notes on the wall around their daughters' names.

Point out that teenage lives intersect with culture much like the Post-it notes come at the names from all directions. Explain that each person is shaped partly by environment. In spite of mothers' concerns or fears, they cannot remove or shield their daughters from the culture in which they live. But they can be aware of the current culture and help their daughters interact in their world with a Christian response.

Say: **During the eight weeks of this study, we will look at major issues facing teenage girls and what we, as mothers, can do to help our daughters in each of these areas. We will also take a close look at our own lives to see what kind of example we are setting for our daughters and to determine if we need to change in order to more clearly reflect our Father and to show His character in our own lives first—before we ask our daughters to live more godly lives.**

Video Viewing

Cue the DVD to the first segment and play it. After the video, spark discussion by asking: **Which of Vicki's stories did you relate to the most? Which truth was most encouraging—that there are no perfect moms, that there are no perfect children, or that there is a perfect God? Why?**

Biblical Mandate

Point out that God's Word is our source for godly living and for teaching our daughters. Invite women in small groups to turn in their Bibles to Deuteronomy 4:1-10. Discuss the passage using questions on pages 16-17 in this book. Invite the women to suggest ways families today pass along spiritual instruction. Say: **All of us are leaving a legacy with our daughters. That's the way it was with the kings of Israel. Some of them were known for good deeds; others for their evil ways. Let's review what we learned about one of the good kings.** Invite women to discuss the life of Josiah by reviewing their responses from pages 17-18. Then say: **Perhaps, as Vicki**

Courtney points out, Josiah did what was right partly because he had a mother who was steering him in the right direction.

Using the book and 2 Kings 22–23, briefly discuss Josiah's example. Include these points: (1) Josiah sought to follow God; (2) He destroyed the idols; (3) He purified and repaired the temple; (4) He repented, renewed the covenant with God, sought to follow God's laws, and led his people to do the same. Ask: **How does Josiah's example speak to us about ways we can be a godly influence for our daughters?**

My Response

Distribute a second set of Post-it® notes. Direct women to write three to five ways they can influence their daughters to live a godly life. Challenge the women to be specific, such as writing "by having a daily quiet time." Invite the women again to place their Post-it® notes on the wall of names.

Say: **Our daughters are bombarded with cultural messages, many of which are negative. In our homes and by our influence, we can add godly direction. With God's help, teens can move through their teenage years doing what is "right in the Lord's sight."**

Gather around the name wall and pray that the influence of godly homes will prepare daughters to deal with cultural clashes. Pray for mothers to provide a Christlike example. Pray for open communication between mothers and daughters and that they will grow in their relationship to each other and to God.

Mother-Daughter Discovery

Challenge the women to use the "Talking Points" at the end of the chapter to talk with their daughters. Suggest that they also share with their daughters some of the temptations they faced as teenagers and some of their greatest fears. Challenge women to allow their daughters to share the temptations and fears that she and her friends face.

Before Next Week

Gather all the Post-it® notes to create two lists: (1) cultural concerns, and (2) godly influences. Note the number of responses of each and be prepared to report the information in session 2.

SESSION 2
Anticonformity

Supplies and Resources

- TV/DVD player
- Posters (made in advance)
- Felt-tip markers
- Bibles
- Pens
- Small chocolates
- Large sheets of paper

Before the Session

- Write "In the world but not of the world" on a large sheet of paper. Write on two sheets of paper "The World's Way" and "God's Way". Place the poster on the focal wall between the two large sheets of paper.
- If you have taken down the poster board with the girls' names, put it back up (without the Post-it notes).
- Arrange chairs in small groups.

Introduction

As women arrive, greet them and direct them to the posters. Invite women to write on the poster labeled "The World's Way" something the world says is acceptable behavior for a teenage girl but may not be a good standard for a Christian. Direct women to write on "God's Way" a quality or behavior that meets God's approval but is not the popular thing to do. Then direct them to take a seat in one of the small groups. Review their responses.

From the last session, share the results of mothers' concerns about their daughters in today's world. Note that many of their concerns would be acceptable norms in today's world. Point out that doing things God's way is often not popular and may mean standing alone. Say: **Helping daughters to stand firm and not to conform is the focus of this session.**

Video Viewing

Play the DVD for this session. Afterward, ask: **What did you think of Vicki's analogy of feasting versus fasting in the world? In what areas is your daughter most tempted to conform? In which areas are you tempted to conform? Thinking back over the story of the teen boy at See You** at the Pole, do you think your daughter would have stood alone at the flagpole? Explain.

Words from Peter

Direct women to find in their Bibles 1 Peter 2:9-12 and read the passage in their small groups. Direct them to review their work from pages 32-33. After several minutes, allow groups to share any insights from discussion. Then say: **When Peter wrote these words, he was offering encouragement to Christians who experienced or risked persecution for being Christ followers.** Ask: **What risks, threats, or dangers do our teenage girls face because they are Christ followers?** Discuss responses.

God's Prized Possession

Say: **Whether our daughters conform will be influenced by how they feel about being Christ followers. And how they feel about being Christ followers will in part depend on your example as a Christ follower.** Invite the women to think of two words to symbolize their life before Christ and their life after Christ. *(Possible answers: lost vs. found; dark vs. light; confusion vs. order; weak vs. strong; broken vs. whole; fear vs. security)* Direct women to write down the words but not to share them yet. While the women are writing, enlist a student to read Romans 6:23.

Because of His Mercy

Direct the women to continue to think about the difference God has made in their lives. Say: **Most of us work hard for what we have. We expect to do that. But we did nothing to earn God's love and mercy. Our salvation came at great cost, but the work was done in love by Jesus Christ in dying for us to save us. We did nothing to earn or deserve that love.**

Ask the student to read Romans 6:23. Explain that God's love paid the price for our sins. Say: **Some of you may have been Christians since you were little girls. You may not often think about the great love gift of God. Others of you may have been a Christ follower for a short time, or this may even be the first time you've heard about God's love. Record your thoughts about such sacrificial love.** Give the women a moment to write in their journals or books.

Because We're His

Ask: **What do you think of when you hear the word *alien*?** Allow for responses, then point out that it simply means people who are in a different place from where they were born, a place they don't call their permanent home. Ask, **If you are a Christ follower, in what way are you an alien?** Affirm their answers. Note that as members of God's kingdom, earth is no longer our permanent address. All aliens feel somewhat at odds with their environment because it is not their permanent home. Christ followers should feel at odds with this world because this is not our home.

A Great Example

Remind the women that the Bible is full of examples of people who were aliens—Ruth, Nehemiah, and Daniel, for example. Invite the women in small groups to list as many facts about Daniel as they can recall without using their Bibles. After groups report, give chocolate to the small group with the longest list. Review Daniel's story using content from page 36-39. Say: **Daniel had a powerful and consistent witness. Regardless of his circumstances, he refused to conform to the culture around him.** Invite women to think about their own witness. Direct them to look at the evaluation tool on page 43-44. Ask: **Do you talk about what it means to be a Christ follower? Have you become too comfortable with the culture? What would your daughter say?**

Closing

Invite women to form a circle. Direct them to think again about the difference Jesus makes in their lives. As a time of praise to God, challenge women to voice the "before and after" words they recorded earlier. Pray for the women, that they will faithfully follow God this week and be an example before their daughters of one who praises and worships God.

Before Next Week

Remind women to check out the "Talking Points" at the end of session 2. Suggest that mothers find a time to get away with daughters during the week. Suggest a trip to a favorite restaurant or a local mall. Also ask women to bring sample teens' and womens' fashion magazines for the next session.

SESSION 3
The Secret of Self-Worth

Supplies and Resources
- Pens
- Bibles
- Teens' and womens' magazines
- TV/DVD player
- Small hand mirrors for women who may not have one
- Poster board

Before the Session
- Arrange chairs in small groups.
- As women arrive, collect the magazines and choose a few whose front covers focus on physical appearance. Display the magazines on a table.
- Prepare a poster board listing the questions for the activity "Worth=Who You Are in Christ."
- Keep the girls' names on the wall.

Introduction
As women arrive, direct them to small groups. Direct women to share in their group three things they like about themselves: (1) physical attributes; (2) a skill, gift, or talent; (3) a personality trait. Explain that they are not allowed to say anything negative about themselves, only positive things. When all have arrived and had opportunity to participate, ask: **Why was this task so difficult?** Explain: **Seeing our own good qualities is difficult; sometimes it seems like bragging. Talking about what we don't like about ourselves is much easier. Hiding from our insecurities and self-doubts is the easiest stance. During this session we'll look at the world's ways of assessing worth. Then we'll discover the real secret of self-worth.** Pause to pray, thanking God for creating these women in His image.

Faulty Formulas for Determining Worth
Direct women to gather in three groups. Assign one "faulty formula" to each group. Tell them that their assignment is to review the information about this fault formula (using the book as a reference), explore the faulty formula, determine how society uses that formula to determine worth,

consider how mothers might also communicate that myth, and what can be done to counteract it. Each group may choose to share their report in a rap; a humorous role play; an on-the-street interview (such as a Jay Leno "Jaywalking" segment); or another creative presentation.

Instruct the "worth=what you look like" group to present its information. After the presentation, ask all the women: **Which of these faulty formulas of self-worth were you trapped by as a teenager? How? How have you bought into the formula that worth=what you look like? How has your daughter bought into that lie? How have you unknowingly (or knowingly) taught your daughter to rely on this faulty foundation for worth? How can you as a mom discourage this fallacy?** Repeat this process for the other two groups of women, pausing to ask the questions above after each presentation. Then say: **Let's view the DVD for this segment to gain further insights into three faulty formulas for self-worth.**

Video Viewing

Cue the DVD to session 3 and play the video. Afterward, ask, **Which of the statistics that Vicki quoted stood out to you the most?** You may want to highlight some of them: Sixty-nine percent of girls surveyed said that magazine pictures influenced their idea of the perfect body. Forty-seven percent of girls wanted to lose weight because of those pictures. Use some of the magazines collected to highlight the emphasis on beauty. Ask: **Does your daughter think she is one diet away from the perfect body? Explain. How have you bought into culture's lie about body image as it relates to our self-worth?** Explain that in one survey, women aged 20-29 and 60-69 had almost the same degree of dissatisfaction with their bodies and wished they could be thinner. Women in the 40-59 age bracket were the most dissatisfied group. Ask: **What does this tell you about the culture's impact on how we view ourselves? Why, then, do we continue to subject ourselves to this unattainable measure of beauty by buying and believing these magazines?** Continue discussing the video by asking: **How are moms most prone to teach their children that worth=what you do? How have you been guilty of garnering your self-worth from your daughter's accomplishments? How can moms foster the faulty idea that worth=what others think of you?**

Worth = Who You Are in Jesus Christ

Explain that the only true place to get our worth is in Christ. Group women into five groups and give each group one of the following Scriptures: Psalm 139:13-17; Isaiah 43:4 1-4; Isaiah 49:15-16; Ephesians 1:4-8; Colossians 1:21-22. (If you break into fewer groups, assign more than one passage to each group.) Direct each group to answer the following questions you have listed on a piece of poster board or dry erase board:

1. What words, phrases or adjectives describe God's children?
2. How might these phrases or adjectives encourage or challenge believers?
3. How do you think your own life would be different if you truly believed what this Scripture says about you?
4. How do you think your daughter's life would be different if she knew and believed what this Scripture says about her?

After several minutes, call on one group to read its Scripture passage, answer the first two questions, and to share any other insights or information they learned from their study together. Then ask the entire large group the last two questions. Repeat this process for the other groups.

Closing

Invite women to get a mirror out of their purses or to take one of the mirrors provided. Ask them all to repeat together after you, a phrase at a time, while looking in the mirror: "I am beautiful. . . . I am wonderfully and fearfully made in God's image. . . . I am loved by the King of the universe. . . . And I am a person of worth." Ask: **How difficult was this exercise? Why?**

To close the session, pray that women will overcome the ways they devalue themselves and the way the world values them. Pray that they will communicate to their daughters that they are secure in God's love and, therefore, persons of great worth.

Before Next Week

Remind mothers of the "Talking Points" at the end of the chapter. Direct them to discuss with their daughters the faulty formulas and which ones they both struggle with. Collect the magazines and use them next week.

SESSION 4
The Pure Life

Supplies and Resources
- Pens
- Bibles
- Cold bottled water for each person
- Women's and teens' magazines
- TV/DVD player

Before the Session
- Arrange the room for five groups.
- Print the team assignments on a large sheet of paper or poster board.
- Keep girls' names on the wall as a silent reminder of the reason for the study.
- Display the magazines. Add to the magazines as needed each week.

Introduction
As women arrive, give each a bottle of cold water. Tell them to enjoy the water and to enjoy a time of fellowship together. Suggest that they share with one another some of the experiences they are having with their daughters using the "Talking Points" at the end of each chapter of the book.

After all have arrived, ask: **Why do we drink bottled water?** *(It's pure; it's healthier than a soda)* **What does the word "pure" mean?** *(clean, uncontaminated)* Say: **It's interesting to think about what things we value in their purest form—water, precious metals, love. It's even more interesting that we value those things as pure, but our culture seems to place little value on a lifestyle of purity, especially sexual purity.**

Share statistics the beginning of this chapter (pp. 65-66). Use the magazines from last week to point out articles about sex, passion, or attraction. Invite women to share shocking evidence of lack of purity in our culture. Caution: Don't let this session get caught up in commenting on the latest shocking scene women have seen on TV, at a movie, or in a magazine. Too much of this is focusing on impurity rather than purity.

Say: **This session focuses on sexual purity, a concept completely foreign to many, laughable to some, old-fashioned to others. In an age when concerns about sex center solely on protection instead of abstinence, it's time to look again at the reasons girls should pursue a life of purity.**

Video Viewing

Cue the DVD to session 4 and play the video. Afterward, ask: **What did you like about Vicki's story of the three brides? How have you tried to communicate to your daughter the importance of sexual purity? What are some practial things you have said or done to try to talk with her about sexual purity?** Say: **We know purity is important, and we want our daughters to pursue purity; but sometimes we don't know how to approach the subject. Let's discover some ways to tackle the issue.**

{ 163 }

Reasons to Wait

Divide women into five groups. Assign to each group one of the reasons girls should wait to have sex until they are married. (See pp. 67-68.) Each group should prepare a report with the following information: (1) The reason to wait until marriage to have sex; (2) What the world says about this reason; (3) What the Bible says; (4) A good way to communicate this reason to teenage girls. Direct women to use their *Your Girl* books, their Bibles, and their own experiences to prepare the reports.

After several minutes, call on groups to report. Then say: **These are good reasons for our daughters to delay having sex until marriage. We can and should tell them about these reasons, these statistics, the consequences of not waiting, and the benefits of waiting. But we must also show them by the lives we live that we really believe what we are saying.**

Living by Your Example

Ask: **What are some practical ways we can demonstrate to our daughters that we are pursuing purity in our own lives—even if we are married?** Say: **The pasages you studied this week provide practical advice for modeling purity before our daughters.** Call on someone to read 1 Corinthians 6:18-20. Ask the group: **How do these verses challenge us to pursue purity in all apsects of our lives? What are some ways we can flee sexual immorality? What is the danger if we don't flee? How do you feel knowing that the Spirit of God lives in you, that you are God's temple?** Call on another woman to read Psalm 101:3. Ask: **What is our challenge, according to this verse? What kinds of things might that include for us?** Read Philippians 4:8. Discuss together the different things Paul challenged believers to focus on. Ask: **How is such a lifestyle different from what you see around you? What unpure things might married mothers of teen daughters focus on? How might those things be detrimental to a woman's marriage and to her daughter?**

If women have not completed the quiz on page 72, direct them to do so at this time. Direct those who have already taken the quiz to look back and to evaluate their own pursuit of purity. Ask the following rhetorical questions: **Was it difficult to be honest? Was it painful to answer the last question truthfully? Did you try to defend your actions? How?** Then say: **It's easy to get caught in the trap of immorality and impurity, even as believers. You must be willing to change your thinking and acting.**

Our Greatest Hope

Lead a brief discussion on ideas for living in the world and remaining pure. Ask: **When sex is used to sell everything from toothpaste to automobiles, when every TV show and movie is full of blatant sex or innuendo and the norm is sex whenever with whomever, how can mothers and daughters remain pure? How can we be examples? How can we help our teenage daughters to value purity?** Use the "Talking Points" on page 75 to begin a discussion. Include ideas about getting fathers involved. Highlight the article "The Role of Fathers in Sexual Purity" on pages 76-77.

Closing

Invite women to spend a few minutes of quiet time reflecting on one or more of the verses you disucssed today and then to use Scripture to write a prayer confessing their own struggles with trying to live a pure life in a sexually explicit and immoral world. After several minutes, say a prayer aloud for the group. Thank God for creating us as sexual beings and pray that we will honor His creation by honoring the marriage relationship. Pray for insight for mothers to be examples for their daughters and to teach them well.

Before Next Week

Remind mothers of the challenges at the end of the chapter. Suggest that, if possible, they get fathers involved this week. Collect the magazines to use next week.

SESSION 5

The Cover Up

Supplies and Resources

- Pens
- Bibles
- Poster board
- Women's and teens' fashion magazines
- Felt-tip markers
- Scissors
- Glue
- TV/DVD player

Before the Session

- Set up the chairs in small groups.
- Keep the girls' names on the wall.
- Arrange the magazines on several tables, depending on your size group.
- Place poster board, scissors, glue, and markers on the tables. Add to the magazine selection with current catalog and newspaper supplements/ads.

  Note: This session includes optional activities requiring advanced planning.

Introduction

As women arrive, direct them to a table to make posters of fashion do's and don'ts using photos from the magazines, ads, and newspaper supplements. The determining factor is modesty. When the women have finished making the posters, display them. Call on a representative of each group to tell about their posters and interpret the do's and don'ts. After all groups have presented their posters, point out that while most mothers are concerned about what their daughters wear, drawing the line is not always easy. Explain that the focus of this session will be on modesty—helping our daughters to honor God, themselves, and the people around them by the way they dress.

Scantily Clad "Role Models"

Ask: **Who are your daughters' role models?** Write these on a whiteboard or chalkboard. Place a check mark by all who are known for their skimpy clothing. Ask: **Does your daughter want to dress like her cultural role models?** Invite mothers to share helpful ways they have assisted their daughters in choosing more appropriate clothing. Lead a discussion on how they have drawn a line about what their daughters can and cannot wear. Ask: **Why do you think some mothers have given up on the battle over purity?**

God's Perspective on Modesty

Direct women in their small groups to turn to Ephesians 5:3-5,8-9; 1 Timothy 2:9-10 and to use the questions on pages 85-86 to guide their discussion of these passages as they relate to modesty. Call on each group to share one insight gained from this study. Be prepared to add to their comments and to summarize using content from your study of the Scriptures and *Your Girl*. Ask: **What excuses does your daughter use for dressing immodestly?** *(it's not really that bad; I want to look fashionable; there's nothing else out there to wear; I don't want to look stupid)* **Do you think it's really possible to dress fashionably and modestly? Why or why not?**

Video Viewing: Living by Example

Say: **As with other topics we've discussed, a mom's example is important. This one may be even more difficult.** Cue the DVD to session 5 and play the video. Afterward, spark discussion by asking: **What did you think of the quote "Sometime over the past couple of decades, while we weren't looking, class went out and trash came in"? What two reasons did Vicki give for why girls dress immodestly?** *(to be fashionable; to be a sex object)* **Which stores do you see carrying the most immodest clothing? Do you allow your daughter to shop there? Why or why not? What was Vicki's challenge for us as mothers when it concerns our dress? Why do you think women our age choose to dress immodestly?** Invite women in their small groups to turn to Romans 14:13-21 and discuss the passage. Encourage moms to talk about their own modesty and what their daughters think of the way they dress.

Teaching Self-Respect

Say: **We set the standard not just by what we wear but also by our confidence and comfort in what we wear. If we obsess about what we wear, we are living in the faulty formula that worth=what we look like. And our daughters are watching. Self-respect means caring about our appearance but at the same time not determining our worth, our daughter's** worth, or the worth of other women, young and old, by what they wear. Ask: **How do we as adult women often judge other women by what they wear? What message does that send to our daughters?** To spin the group discussion in another direction, ask, **What would you do if your daughter brought home a friend who dressed very immodestly?**

Encourage moms to talk with daughters about what they value most in life and how they choose their friends and acquaintances. Where do clothing and other material possessions fall on this list? Are their daughters willing to be friends with someone who doesn't dress fashionably? Who doesn't dress modestly? This can be a teachable moment for both moms and daughters.

Setting the Standards

Direct women in their small groups to review the standards suggested on page 92. Do they have standards of their own to add? Do they disagree with any of these? Allow time to add or argue different ideas and perspectives.

What's a Mother or Daughter to Do?

Review the activist ideas noted in *Your Girl*. Ask whether anyone in your group has confronted a store about appropriate clothing. Is such confrontation needed in your community? Are there women who want to do this together? Help women who want to take an active stance to meet together after the session. Don't spend a lot of time during the session working out these details. Also discuss ways girls can speak out in favor of modest fashions. Encourage mothers to let their daughters work for positive change.

Closing

Gather around the names wall again. Invite mothers to voice sentence prayers for themselves and their daughters, asking God for strength to stand against immodesty and to honor God and others by the way they dress.

Before Next Week

Suggest that mothers and daughters go shopping together to talk about appropriate dress. Encourage mothers to listen more than lecture.

SESSION 6

Prince Charming: Fact or Fairy Tale?

Supplies and Resources
- TV/DVD player
- Bibles of various translations
- Chalkboard or dry erase board

Before the session
- Set up the chairs in small groups.
- Keep the girls' names on the wall.
- Write or type the following Scripture references and enlist women to be prepared to read them: Deuteronomy 33:26-27; Psalm 13:5-6; Psalm 130:7; Psalm 136; Isaiah 54:10; Lamentations 3:22-23; Zephaniah 3:17; Romans 8:38-39; 1 John 3:16; 1 John 4:9-10; 1 John 4:18; and Revelation 1:5b-6.
- Prepare slips of paper for the activity in the Introduction.
- Make a poster of Ephesians 3:17-19 with a blank space where the word "you" is, as shown on page 110.

Introduction

Play a game of Pictionary. Explain that volunteers will draw the names of movies. Write the following movie titles on separate slips of paper and put them in a container: *Pretty Woman, You've Got Mail, Last of the Mohicans, Runaway Bride, Notting Hill; What a Girl Wants; An Affair to Remember, Sleepless in Seattle*. Take turns playing the game. Then ask: **What did all of these movies have in common? What is your favorite romantic or "happily-ever-after" movie? Why are these movies so popular with women?** Say: **These movies are fun and fantasy, and we all know that after they ride into the sunset, the loving couple will have to face all the realities of life. These movies can be a great escape, but generally they are not very realistic.** Explain that helping their daughters set high but not unrealistic standards for the man they will date and/or marry is the focus of this session.

Video Viewing

Cue the DVD to session 6. Before playing the video, ask: **How have you** seen dating and courtship change from your generation to this generation? Say, **Today's video highlights the changes that our daughters face in today's world.** Play the video. Afterward, ask: **What stood out to you in this video? What surprised, shocked, alarmed, or encouraged you? How can we teach our daughters to develop a high standard for dating without setting them up for disappointment?**

The Desire for Happily Ever After

Direct women to turn in their Bibles to Proverbs 19:22a. Call on women to read it in various translations. Say: **Despite the dating practices today, girls still hope to find that one true love, a love that will be faithful. One reason we like romantic movies is the appeal of a faithful love, one that will last, will not disappoint or betray.** Tell the Jerry McGuire story from *Your Girl*. Say: **Unfortunately, no man can meet fairy-tale expectations. Many teenage girls are looking for Prince Charming when most guys are more like Shrek—lovable, real, and good-intentioned, but flawed nonetheless. So what's the answer? Only One can truly make us complete, fill the hole in our hearts, make us feel completely loved—and that one is Jesus.**

The Filler of Our Hearts

Call on a woman to read Ephesians 1:4-5. Give small groups a few minutes to discuss the questions on pages 102-103. Say: **Teenage girls are not the only ones who try to fill a void in their lives with a human relationship or something else that substitutes for God. It is a human malady known to all.** Ask: **What are some things people use to try to fill the void in their lives? If God's love is so great, then why do we often accept a cheap substitute?**

Call on the previously enlisted women to stand at random and to read their Scripture selections. After all have read, summarize by pointing out that the Bible is full of God's love for us. From Genesis to Revelation—from creation to the second coming—God has shown His love for us. Nothing on earth can come close to equaling His love.

Knowing the Unknowable

Say, **Instead of looking for love in all the wrong places, we should praise**

God for His costly love poured out for us. Keep women in their small groups. Direct them to turn in their Bibles to Ephesians 3:17-19 and to use the questions on page 105-106 to discuss the verses. Invite groups to respond with truths and observations from their discussions. Summarize by saying, **Only God's love completes us, but a guy and a girl who are both secure in their love for God and in His love for them have a great foundation for building a solid relationship with each other.**

Learning the Lesson Early
Invite mothers to share their experiences of talking with their daughters about dating, relationships with guys, and marriage. Focus on discussions about relationships—expectations, criteria for serious relationships, and so forth. Mothers of younger girls may want to ask questions of women with older teen daughters. Keep the conversation from getting bogged down, but allow some time for this if there is a good exchange of helpful ideas.

Love and Marriage
Invite the women to reflect on the ways they have tried to equip their daughters for a dating (and ultimately marriage) relationship. More than likely some women in the group will have experienced multiple marriages or are single mothers, and many may feel they have failed in this area. Point out that in all areas mothers are fallible, including this one. But all mothers can continue to teach their daughters God's love that will not fail. Also discuss ways mothers can model healthy marital relationships for their daughters to see.

Closing
Invite women to stand together where they can see the names wall as well as Ephesians 3:17-19. Direct them to read this in unison as their closing prayer, each mother saying aloud her daughter(s) name to fill in the blank.

Before Next Week
Remind women of the "Talking Points." Suggest that they consider letting their daughters choose a "happily-ever-after" movie for the two of them to watch. Complete the time together with a realistic discussion of love and "happily ever after."

SESSION 7
Girl Politics

Supplies and Resources
- TV/DVD player
- Bibles
- Small chocolates

Before the Session
- Set up the chairs in small groups.
- Keep the girls' names on the wall.

   Note: This session includes optional activities requiring advanced planning.

Introduction

As women arrive, direct them to small groups. Direct them to list TV shows or movies in which being mean to another person is an essential part of the plot. (Most reality shows have this element.) After everyone has arrived and had opportunity to participate, review the TV show lists. Point out that being mean to one another has now become a celebrated and rewarded part of our cultural norm. Say: **Girls have long been known to be mean to one another during the teen years and beyond, but in today's world being mean has risen to a whole new level.** Allow women to share a time when they were deeply hurt by girl politics. Then explain that dealing with "girl politics" and how to get along in a mean world is this session's focus.

   Option: As women arrive, play short clips from the movie *Mean Girls* to show different ways girls are mean to one another.

Video Viewing

Cue the video to session 7 and play it. Afterward, ask: **Which examples of girl politics surprised you? How has your daughter been involved in girl politics? Why do you think girls are especially prone to engage in issues such as cliques, gossip, jealousy, and blatant meanness? Is it comforting to know that girl politics were around even in biblical times? Why or why not? What did you think about Vicki's story about St. Francis of Assisi? How does this story apply to our discussion today? How does her ending quote apply to our discussion?**

Cliques

Ask: **What cliques did you encounter or were a part of in junior high and high school? Do you think cliques are different for your teen girl now than they were for you as a teen? How would you define a clique?** If you have time, review the questions on page 119. Say: **Cliques are ages-old girl groups. They are groups that purposely exclude others and act superior to everyone else.** Assign the Scriptures on page 120 to five different groups (if you have enough participants). Direct someone from various teams to read the verse and begin the discussion of this Scripture as it relates to cliques. Suggest that everyone take notes as Scriptures are discussed.

Ask: **Is there a difference between a clique and a group of girlfriends? If so, what? How can we encourage our girls to develop healthy friendships without being exclusive? How are cliques different for us as mothers? What cliques do you see women in? Why do you think women are drawn to cliques? How have you been on the negative end of a clique, even as an adult?** Challenge women to think about their relationships with other women. Do they exclude others? If so, what do they need to do about it?

Gossip

Say: **We were told when we were children that "sticks and stones may break my bones, but words will never hurt me." Even as we used to say these words, we knew they were not true. Words do hurt, and gossip is one way words can hurt us. God must have known how much trouble we would have with our tongues, for the Bible has much to say about our words.**

Keep women in groups and assign the following Scripture groups: Proverbs 10:19; Proverbs 16:28; Romans 1:29-31; James 1:26; James 3:9. Direct women to discuss these Scriptures and report their findings. Ask: **How do girls tend to talk to each other?** *(face-to-face conversation, blogs, instant messaging, e-mails, text messaging, over the phone)* **Why do you think these are such popular methods for gossip?** Explain that some people will type nasty stuff or innuendoes that they'd never say in person.

Jealousy

Say, **Jealousy may not at first appear to be a tool for girls to be mean to** one another, but a girl who is jealous may act out in hurtful ways because of her emotions. Assign the Scriptures on pages 125-126, one per group. Allow time for women to discuss the passage using the questions provided. Then ask volunteers to share with the large group while everyone takes notes. Ask: **How do you see jealousy manifest itself most often in your daughter's life? How might your family's behavior actually foster feelings of jealousy?** Challenge the women to consider their own jealousy by reviewing the checklist on page 126. Ask: **Were you surprised by the things that spark jealousy in you? What things do you do to keep your jealousy in check?**

Our Example

Say: **We've been talking a lot about how our teen girls struggle with girl politics. The truth of the matter is that we struggle with it just as much as they do. Sometimes, they have learned from our example when that example isn't good! This is certainly one area we don't outgrow.**

Direct the women to spend a few moments in quiet reflection, perhaps focusing on one of the verses studied today. Challenge the women to think about the area (cliques, jealousy, gossip) in which they need God's help and to choose a verse from today's discussion that speaks to that problem area. Direct women to write down the verse and keep it where they can see it during the next week.

Closing

Direct the women to gather around the names wall, touching the names. If necessary, do this in more than one group. Challenge them to offer a silent prayer for their own daughters and the other girls on the wall that they will neither hurt others by what they say and do or be hurt by such actions. Pray that when hurts come their way, they will overcome them by God's love.

Before Next Week

Remind women of the "Talking Points." Suggest that mothers try e-mailing messages to their daughters—encouraging them, writing prayers for them, and sharing information. They should not stop real conversation, but it can be a fun way to add another dimension to their relationships.

SESSION 8
Leaving a Heritage

Supplies and Resources
- Pens
- Bibles
- Small chocolates
- A small, smooth stone for each participant (available at crafts stores and gardening centers)
- TV/DVD player

Before the Session
- Set up the chairs in small groups.
- Keep the girls' names on the wall.

   Note: This session includes an optional activity requiring advanced planning.

Introduction

When women come in, give them a small, smooth stone and direct them to take a seat in one of the small groups. Direct small groups to list all the things you can do, both good and bad, with different kinds of rocks. After all of the women have arrived, review the list. Give a prize to the small group with the longest list. Direct women to keep their rocks.

Say: **Just as rocks can hurt, destroy, or build up, mothers have that same power with their daughters. Both intentionally—by the ways you seek to teach your daughter(s), and accidentally—by the example you set in everything you say and do, you influence your girls. Then they, too, have power for both positive and negative thoughts and actions. But one thing is sure: if we can teach our daughters to build on the Rock, the solid foundation of Jesus Christ, they will have what they need to build their life for Him.**

Video Viewing: The Heritage of God's Word

Cue the DVD to session 8. Say: **To build their lives on the solid foundation of Jesus Christ, our daughters need to be familiar with God's Word. There is no substitute, no condensed version.** Play the video segment. Afterward, ask: **What is most challenging for you as a mother trying to impart biblical truths to your daughter? What hinders you from depending on God's Word as your source of strength, guidance, and direction?**

Why do you think we take God's Word for granted? Why do you think our daughters choose not to look to it as the standard for their lives? Lead women to reflect on their own godly heritage. **Did someone leave a heritage of faith to you, much like Vicki's grandmother left one to her? If so, whom?** Invite a few women to volunteer a response.

Say: **One theologian, before preaching at a seminary, read his sermon text from the Bible. After he read the verses, he said, "These words are true; you can trust them."** Ask: **Do you truly believe that God's Word is trustworthy? Why or why not? If we view God's Word as trustworthy and reliable, then why do we choose not to live by it?** Say: **In our culture, it's hard to find something that's trustworthy, reliable, and absolute truth. It's good to remind ourselves when we read God's Word that His Word is true.**

Option: Enlist a biblical scholar or layperson familiar with apologetics to talk about different kinds of proof that the Bible is reliable.

The Heritage of Prayer

Say: **A heritage of God's Word is important, but it is also important for our daughters to learn the heritage of prayer—the crying out of our hearts before Him.** Briefly review the ACTS prayer model as described on pages 134-137. Ask: **Have any of you used this prayer model in your own relationship with God?** If some have used this model, encourage them to share how this model has impacted their relationship with God. Ask: **After reading about this ACTS model, is there an area of your prayer life that needs more attention? Explain.** Also allow women to share other models of prayer they use. Ask: **How can we teach our daugthers the importance of prayer? What are some ways you have modeled prayer for your daughter? Does your daughter know you pray for her on a consistent basis? Explain.**

Remind women that conversation means listening as well as talking—something we sometimes have to remember when talking with God and with our daughters. Say, **Our goal is twofold: to improve our own prayer life and the way we pray for our daughters and also to pass on to them a legacy of worship and prayer.** Spend a few minutes brainstorming ways to set the standard for a life of praise and prayer. Allow women to work in groups and report their ideas to the large group.

Top 10 Faith Compromisers

Say: **A heritage of prayer and God's Word are essential. So is a heritage of faith.** Call attention to the Top 10 Faith Compromisers on pages 140-147. Assign each of these to a group. Some small groups may have to work on more than one, or you may ask women to work in pairs. Assign a faith compromiser to each group. Direct pairs or groups to review the content and tell the entire group their faith compromiser and how mothers can, if needed, confront this situation. Let the emphasis be on positive, creative ways to avoid the faith compromisers. Ask: **If you're willing to share, what faith compromiser has been a struggle for you or your family? How have you tried to deal with it?**

Closing

Say: **Over these eight weeks, you have probably build relationships with others in this group. Find ways to continue to support one another. Talk often. Get together. Pray for one another. You have probably also gained new insight and renewed passion for raising your girl to be a godly young woman. Continue on that journey. Review "Talking Points" and try new ways to teach, train, and talk with your girl. And finally, take the stones home with you. Place them where you will see them every day. Let them be a small altar for you, a reminder as in biblical times of God's good-ness and your desire to build your life and your daughter's on the solid foundation of Jesus Christ. When you see the stone, pray for your girl.**

Direct women refert to pages 138-139 for a list of Christian attributes to pray for their teen girls. Instruct women to choose one specific attribute they want to pray for their daugthers as they close out this study. Then call the women to the name wall again. Explain that this closing prayer time will include a chance for them to offer up a prayer for their daughter. After women have had the opportunity to voice their prayers, close the Bible study by thanking God for this time together. Pray for mothers who want to raise daughters to be like their Heavenly Father, for daughters to grow in the grace and knowledge of God.